Carthaginian Armies of the Punic Wars, 264–146 BC

Gabriele Esposito is a military historian who works as a freelance author and researcher for some of the most important publishing houses in the military history sector. In particular, he is an expert specializing in uniformology: his interests and expertise range from the ancient civilizations to modern post-colonial conflicts. During recent years he has conducted and published several researches on the military history of the Latin American countries, with special attention on the War of the Triple Alliance and the War of the Pacific. He is among the leading experts on the military history of the Italian Wars of Unification and the Spanish Carlist Wars. His books and essays are published on a regular basis by Pen & Sword Books, Osprey Publishing, Winged Hussar Publishing and Libreria Editrice Goriziana, and he is also the author of numerous military history articles appearing in specialized magazines such as *Ancient Warfare Magazine*, *Medieval Warfare Magazine*, *The Armourer*, *History of War*, *Guerres et Histoire*, *Focus Storia* and *Focus Storia Wars*.

Carthaginian Armies of the Punic Wars, 264–146 BC

History, Organization and Equipment

Gabriele Esposito

Pen & Sword
MILITARY

First published in Great Britain in 2023 by
Pen & Sword Military
An imprint of
Pen & Sword Books Limited
Yorkshire – Philadelphia

Copyright © Gabriele Esposito 2023

ISBN 978 1 39906 754 6

The right of Gabriele Esposito to be identified as
Author of this Work has been asserted by him in accordance
with the Copyright, Designs and Patents Act 1988.

A CIP catalogue record for this book is
available from the British Library

Typeset by Mac Style
Printed and bound in India by Replika Press Pvt. Ltd.

Pen & Sword Books Limited incorporates the imprints of After the Battle,
Atlas, Archaeology, Aviation, Discovery, Family History, Fiction, History,
Maritime, Military, Military Classics, Politics, Select, Transport, True Crime,
Air World, Frontline Publishing, Leo Cooper, Remember When, Seaforth
Publishing, The Praetorian Press, Wharncliffe Local History, Wharncliffe
Transport, Wharncliffe True Crime and White Owl.

For a complete list of Pen & Sword titles please contact

PEN & SWORD BOOKS LIMITED
47 Church Street, Barnsley, South Yorkshire, S70 2AS, England
E-mail: enquiries@pen-and-sword.co.uk
Website: www.pen-and-sword.co.uk
or
PEN AND SWORD BOOKS
1950 Lawrence Rd, Havertown, PA 19083, USA
E-mail: uspen-and-sword@casematepublishers.com
Website: www.penandswordbooks.com

Contents

Acknowledgements

This book is dedicated to my magnificent parents, Maria Rosaria and Benedetto, for the immense love and fundamental support that they always give me. Their precious advice has helped make this book even better than I had hoped. A very special thanks goes to Philip Sidnell, the commissioning editor of my books for Pen & Sword: his love for history and his passion for publishing are key factors behind the success of our publications. Many thanks also to the production manager of this title, Matt Jones, for his excellent work and great enthusiasm. A special mention is due to Tony Walton for the magnificent work of editing that he carries out for all my books. A very special mention goes to the brilliant re-enactment groups that collaborated with their photographs to the creation of this book: without the incredible work of research by their members, the final result of this publication would have not been the same. As a result, I want to express my deep gratitude to the following living history associations: Make Carthage Great Again from France (in the person of Denis Taverne); Terra Carpetana from Spain; Hetairoi from Germany; Confraternita del Leone/Historia Viva, Antichi Popoli and Insubria Gaesata from Italy.

Introduction

Among the military forces of Antiquity, the Carthaginian Army is without doubt among the most difficult to study. Soon after its creation, it began to have a very 'multi-ethnic' nature, comprising warriors coming from every corner of the Mediterranean. Carthage, the most important of the colonies founded by the Phoenicians, rapidly became the greatest naval power of Antiquity, establishing a commercial empire that extended over most of the Mediterranean. Its citizens, however, did not consider military expansion as their primary activity: they preferred investing in trading and wherever possible tried to avoid the outbreak of major conflicts. Over time, however, Carthaginian interests in the Mediterranean began colliding with those of the Greeks and – some centuries later – the Romans. The Carthaginian commercial outposts needed to be defended to continue flourishing, and simply having an impressive fleet was not enough to do so. As a result, Carthage started to expand its military forces, recruiting large numbers of mercenaries from the various warrior peoples of the western Mediterranean. By the beginning of the first conflict fought against Rome, the Carthaginian Army already comprised a majority of mercenaries, supported by a minority of 'national' troops. This trend continued during the following decades, which saw the Carthaginians trying to eliminate the ascending power of the Roman Republic during the three Punic Wars. These conflicts derived their name from the term that the Romans used to indicate the Carthaginians, *Punici*. At the beginning of the First Punic War, the military forces of Carthage consisted of three main components: the national Carthaginian and Liby-Phoenician troops, the allied/vassal troops provided by the Numidians and other indigenous peoples of northern Africa, and the mercenary soldiers recruited by the Carthaginian colonies in Iberia (modern Spain and Portugal) and Sardinia. The Carthaginian citizen troops consisted of an elite corps – the Sacred Band – and numerous other specialist elements, including their officers and war elephants. The Liby-Phoenicians were far more numerous, originating from a mixed population that had emerged from encounters between the Carthaginians and the Libyans. These 'provincial' Carthaginians provided the bulk of the Carthaginian Army's heavy infantry, from the First Punic War onwards being equipped in Hellenistic fashion as phalangites. The allied/vassal troops provided by the Berber peoples of northern Africa, who were not proper mercenaries since their communities were part of Carthage's sphere of influence, made up the light cavalry and light infantry of the Carthaginian Army. The Iberians and Sardinians were true mercenaries, being hired in large numbers by the Carthaginians from some of the Mediterranean's most warlike tribes. Between the First Punic War and the Second Punic War, Carthage established its indirect political/commercial control over most of Iberia, in consequence of which large numbers of Iberian mercenaries were recruited in the region. These soon became the backbone of Hannibal's victorious army that invaded the Italian peninsula and defeated the Romans in several major pitched battles. The Iberians provided heavy infantry, light infantry, heavy cavalry, light cavalry and elite Balearic slingers. During the Second Punic War, another two categories of foreign troops were added to the Carthaginian Army: Celtic and Italic warriors. After crossing the Alps, Hannibal entered northern Italy – called *Gallia Cisalpina* by the Romans – a region that had long been inhabited by numerous Celtic tribes. The latter had recently been submitted by the Roman Republic and still resented their rule. Consequently, when the Carthaginians invaded Italy, the Celts of Cisalpine Gaul joined the Carthaginian Army en masse as mercenaries. They served as heavy infantry and heavy cavalry, being second only to the Iberians in terms of numerical and tactical importance. Hannibal was also perceived as a liberator by many of the Italic peoples who had been defeated and subjugated by the Romans before the First Punic War. The most warlike and numerous of these, known as the Oscan Peoples, soon joined the Carthaginians in their struggle against Rome. The Ligures of north-western Italy, whose territories were crossed on several occasions by Carthaginian troops, also joined Hannibal. Many Oscan warriors remained loyal to the Carthaginians even after Hannibal left Italy, and served under his orders at the Battle of Zama. In this book we will provide an overview of the military campaigns fought by Carthage during the Punic Wars, while also describing in detail the organization, equipment and tactics of the various contingents that made up the Carthaginian Army.

Chapter 1

The Early History of Carthage and its Military Forces

History and organization

The city of Carthage was founded in 814 BC on the coastline on North Africa, not far from present-day Tunis. Its founders were the Phoenicians, a people of merchants and sailors originating from modern Lebanon who had been masters of the Mediterranean's naval commerce for many centuries. The ninth century BC, the historical period during which Carthage was built, was a time of great change for the Mediterranean world. After the so-called Dark Ages that followed the collapse of the Bronze Age and its great civilizations, the Greeks and Phoenicians started to navigate the Mediterranean Sea to spread their new cultures and enlarge their mercantile networks by creating colonies in distant lands. These Greek or Phoenician colonies were urban centres located on the coastline with a distinct commercial nature, acting as bases for the merchants who had sponsored their foundation but also as a gathering point for those Greeks or Phoenicians who wished to leave their homeland in search of new opportunities abroad. Since the Middle East was dominated by great empires such as that of the Assyrians, the Greeks and Phoenicians looked westwards in search of new regions to colonize, aiming for Italy, southern France, Iberia and northern Africa. Inhabited by warlike peoples but rich in precious natural resources, these areas around the Mediterranean appeared perfect for commercial penetration by the seafaring peoples from Greece and Phoenicia. The Greeks, who created their own alphabet by following the innovative example of the Phoenicians, directed their efforts towards southern Italy, whereas the Phoenicians turned their attention towards North Africa. The Phoenicians, like the Greeks, were not organized as a single kingdom in their homeland of Phoenicia, instead being politically fragmented into a series of fully autonomous city-states. These were quite weak from a military point of view – since they could not field large armies – but were incredibly rich thanks to commerce. Their agile ships were the most modern vessels travelling across the Mediterranean, transporting luxury goods produced in the Middle East to the new markets of the western Mediterranean. Thanks to their superior naval capabilities, the Phoenician sailors were able to reach every corner of an Ancient World that was still in the process of being explored.

Officer of the Carthaginian Army wearing Phrygian helmet and scale cuirass. (*Photo and copyright by Denis Taverne of Make Carthage Great Again*)

For several decades, the Phoenician cities – the most important of which were Tyre and Sydon – flourished economically and were able to preserve their independence. It was during this period that Carthage and most of the other Phoenician colonies were created, not only in northern Africa but also in the major islands of southern Italy. During the central decades of the eighth century BC, however, the great territorial expansion of the warlike Assyrian Empire began to menace Phoenicia. By 738 BC, all the Phoenician cities had been occupied by the Assyrians or been transformed into vassal states. After the collapse of the Assyrian Empire, the Phoenicians failed to regain their previous autonomy, first being submitted by the Neo-Babylonian Empire and then by the Persian Empire of Cyrus the Great. Following the conquest of Assyrian lands, the Phoenicians gradually lost all the character that had permitted them to create a commercial empire across the Mediterranean, and several of their mercantile outposts were attacked by the Greeks. The fall of Phoenicia, however, did not cause the decline of Carthage and the other Phoenician colonies. After the destruction of Tyre by the Babylonians, the Carthaginians, whose city had been founded by colonists from Tyre, gradually replaced their motherland as the leading commercial centre of the Mediterranean Sea, expanding their fleet in a massive way. Following these events, several Phoenician colonies that had previously been independent were obliged to acknowledge Carthage's overlordship. It is thus possible to say that the rapid rise of Carthage was greatly aided by the difficulties experienced by the Phoenicians in the Middle East. The Carthaginians thereby became the main heirs of the empire created by their Phoenician ancestors, soon assuming a leading role in the political scene of the western Mediterranean. Here, there were no major urban centres that could compete with Carthage on equal terms, apart from the rich Greek colonies of Sicily and mainland southern Italy.

The expansionism of the Greeks caused great concerns among the minor colonies founded by the Phoenicians in the western Mediterranean, so several of them quite happily accepted becoming Carthaginian vassals in exchange for receiving the emerging naval power's protection. The Carthaginians, thanks to their massive naval and economic resources, were able to establish several new commercial bases across the Mediterranean in order to limit the expansionism of the Greeks – in Malta, western Sicily, Sardinia, Corsica, the Balearic Islands and Iberia. The Carthaginians also expanded their control along the coastline of northern Africa by absorbing all the various Phoenician colonies already existing in the region, as well as by colonizing new lands in Algeria and Libya. Around 520 BC, Carthage sent a large fleet across the Straits of Gibraltar – which marked the end of the known world for the Greeks – with the objective of founding new colonies on the western coastline of Morocco. The Carthaginian sailors, by following the African coast, moved south and reached the Gulf

Officer of the Carthaginian Army armed with *falcata* sword. (*Photo and copyright by Denis Taverne of Make Carthage Great Again*)

Officer of the Carthaginian Navy wearing a linothorax cuirass reinforced with brass scales. (*Photo and copyright by Denis Taverne of Make Carthage Great Again*)

of Guinea, where, in modern Senegal, they established various temporary outposts from which the products of the African hinterland could be exported to the Mediterranean. The new colonies created by Carthage were inhabited by the surplus population of the city, which was becoming too numerous. Marriages between Carthaginians and native Africans started to be extremely common, and thus a new people emerged in northern Africa: the Liby-Phoenicians, who inhabited the countryside surrounding Carthage as well as the Carthaginian colonies located on the North African coastline.

From 580 BC, a series of incidents began to take place between the Carthaginians and Greeks along the coastline of Italy, which erupted into full-scale war around 540 BC. The Carthaginians had allied themselves with the most powerful of the Italic peoples, the Etruscans, the main regional rivals of the Greek colonists in Italy who had previously dominated the commercial routes that crossed the Italian peninsula. At the Battle of Alalia (*c.*540 BC), a joint Etruscan-Carthaginian fleet was crushed by warships sent by the rich Greek colony of Cumae, which obtained a great victory in Corsican waters. Following this naval clash, the Etruscans ceased to be a significant naval power, meaning the Carthaginians had to search for a new ally. In 509 BC, the senate of Carthage concluded an alliance with a little-known city that was emerging as the leading regional power of central Italy: Rome. The latter had just become a republic after having long been dominated by Etruscan kings, and was in search of a powerful ally with notable commercial capabilities. The newly born Roman Republic, still under the potential menace of the Etruscans, was in search of overseas recognition, whereas Carthage needed an Italic ally in order to limit the expansionism of the Greeks in southern Italy and Sicily. In 480 BC, hoping to take advantage of the Persian invasion of mainland Greece, the Carthaginians organized a massive military expedition against Sicily with the objective of conquering the whole island. At that time, the dominant military power of Sicily was the city of Syracuse, Carthage controlling only the westernmost portion of the island. The ensuing conflict, known as the First Sicilian War, ended in complete failure for the Carthaginians when they were soundly defeated at the Battle of Himera. During this clash, the superiority of the Syracusan cavalry – together with the perfect drill of the Greek hoplites – proved a decisive factor. For the following seventy years, Carthage organized no further expeditions against the Greeks of Sicily, limiting itself to the defence of its colonies located in the western part of the island. During this period, the Carthaginians founded new commercial settlements in Iberia and conducted a major exploration of the Sahara that took them as far as the eastern borders of Egypt. A rejuvenated Carthage then embarked on the Second Sicilian War from 410–404 BC. This saw a series of Carthaginian victories in the initial stages, but these were not decisive as they were not achieved against the major Greek cities of Syracuse and Akragas. During the second phase of the conflict, the Carthaginians besieged Akragas, but their troops were ravaged by plague and experienced serious difficulties before finally being able to capture the city. By the end of the Second Sicilian War, Carthaginian power had reached its peak in Sicily, with several local cities having accepted their formal suzerainty.

After a brief pause, the Third Sicilian War broke out, continuing from 398– 393 BC, the Carthaginians intervening again against Syracuse in order to limit the expansionist ambitions of the Sicilian city's dictator, Dionysius. Carthaginian forces besieged Syracuse after obtaining a great naval victory at the Battle of Catana, but were again ravaged by plague and had to abandon the siege when it had seemed likely they were about to capture the city. By the end of the conflict, the situation on the island had changed very little and a treaty was signed between the two warring parties, dividing Sicily into two spheres of influence dominated by Carthage and Syracuse. However, tensions continued and led to the Fourth Sicilian War (383– 376 BC). This began with several victories for Carthage, which had been able to form an anti-Syracuse alliance with the Greek colony of Taras in mainland southern Italy and various other Italic peoples. In 376 BC, the Carthaginians destroyed a Syracusan army at the Battle of Cronium, which brought the conflict to a decisive close. The subsequent peace treaty forced Dionysius of Syracuse to pay a huge sum of money to Carthage, but this failed to prevent the Fifth Sicilian War breaking out in 368 BC when Syracuse attacked Carthaginian possessions in Sicily and laid siege to their most important Sicilian colony, the fortified city of Lilybaeum. Dionysius, however, died during the conflict and was succeeded by his son, Dionysius II, who preferred to make peace with the Carthaginians in 367 BC. Nevertheless, the peace was again short-lived, and the Sixth Sicilian War of 345–339 BC saw the Carthaginians taking advantage of Syracuse's internal political divisions. However, in the last year of the conflict the Syracusans were able to obtain a great victory at the Battle of the Crimissus, following which the Halcyas River started to mark the border between the territorial possessions of Carthage and Syracuse in Sicily. The Seventh Sicilian War (311–306 BC) began with a series of victories for the armies of Syracuse, which were guided by the city's new tyrant, Agathocles. He occupied most of the Carthaginian colonies in Sicily and laid siege to the important city of Akragas. However, Carthage struck back, organizing an effective counter-attack and defeating Agathocles at the Battle of the Himera River. When Carthaginian forces in Sicily then besieged Syracuse, a desperate Agathocles responded by sending an army of 14,000 men to North Africa to threaten the city of Carthage. Agathocles' strategic vision bore fruit, since the Carthaginian forces besieging Syracuse were recalled to defend their homeland. Against all odds, the Greek expeditionary force then won a great pitched battle outside Carthage, after which Agathokles laid siege to the enemy city but could not gain entry as Carthage was too strongly fortified. After campaigning for two years in Tunisia, the forces of Syracuse were finally defeated and had to abandon their expedition. These events marked the end of the long series of Sicilian Wars, which had started in 480 BC. Nevertheless, it would not be long before Pyrrhus of Epirus campaigned in Sicily from 278–276 BC to support the local Greeks in their struggle against Carthage. The great warrior king Pyrrhus obtained a series of important victories that expelled Carthaginian troops from the whole of Sicily except for their stronghold of Lilybaeum, which he besieged without success. Pyrrhus then returned to mainland southern Italy, where he was later defeated by the Romans, and the status quo was restored in Sicily.

The city of Carthage was ruled by a senate and a popular assembly. The senate consisted of 300 aristocrats, who were nobles by wealth rather than birth. Its members – known as shofets or suffetes – controlled civil administration in an oligarchic way and could be re-elected without limits. A permanent inner council of thirty nobles – chosen from the most prominent members of the senate – was tasked with electing the supreme commanders of the army and the navy. Each of the commanders was always accompanied by a deputy from the senate in order to avoid the outbreak of military rebellions. The inner council was later expanded to comprise 104 members and became increasingly important. The popular assembly consisted of

Carthaginian infantry officer wearing Montefortino helmet and scale cuirass. (*Photo and copyright by Denis Taverne of Make Carthage Great Again*)

all the Carthaginian citizens possessing a certain qualification in property; it ratified the election of the shofets but had very little practical power. Since its foundation, Carthage had a citizen militia for home defence, which was raised only in time of need and thus was a temporary military force. The Carthaginians, being merchants and craftsmen, did not consider war as a profitable activity since it could cause enormous damage to their commercial enterprises. When possible, Carthage thus always tried to avoid new conflicts against its enemies; but when war was inevitable, the Carthaginians were prone to recruiting large numbers of foreign mercenaries to fight in their place. The production and buying and selling of goods could not be stopped, even in time of war, so it was quite natural to pay professional soldiers from abroad to conduct military campaigns in order to avoid the economic problems that could have derived from the formation of a citizen army. By the fifth century BC, the old citizen militia – which could muster around 45,000 heavy infantrymen – could be mobilized only in time of extreme crisis. This happened several times during the period taken into account: when Agathokles besieged Carthage, during the Great Mercenary Revolt that took place after the end of the First Punic War, when Scipio Africanus invaded North Africa at the end of the Second Punic War and during the final siege of Carthage during the Third Punic War. In times of peace or of conflicts fought abroad, the only permanent military force entirely made up of Carthaginian soldiers was the Sacred Band. This was an elite military corps, which was very similar to the 'epilektoi' units of contemporary Greek cities, consisting of 2,500 young men drawn from the richest families of Carthage. The Sacred Band acted as an elite heavy infantry corps equipped in Hellenic fashion, but also as a training unit. Its young members, after leaving the corps, became the officers of the Carthaginian Army. The various contingents of foreign mercenaries had their own officers, but each of them was placed under the overall command of a Carthaginian superior officer. In consequence, for offensive operations as well as for defence, Carthage relied almost entirely on hired mercenaries or on soldiers levied from its vassals and allies. The Carthaginians had plenty of money, since they exacted tributes from all their colonies and from the native tribes living around those settlements. Tributes could also be paid in kind, especially in those areas that were rich in natural resources and mines, such as Iberia. Each contingent of foreign mercenaries in Carthaginian service fought in its own way and following its own military traditions, as a result of which the success of Carthaginian arms largely depended on their generals' ability to hold the various detachments together and to use their different tactical capabilities in the best possible way.

The Libyans, on whose land Carthage had been erected, were soon reduced to the status of free tributary cultivators by the Carthaginians, being required to yield

Carthaginian heavy infantryman
equipped in Hellenistic fashion, with
linothorax cuirass and hoplon shield.
(*Photo and copyright by Denis Taverne of
Make Carthage Great Again*)

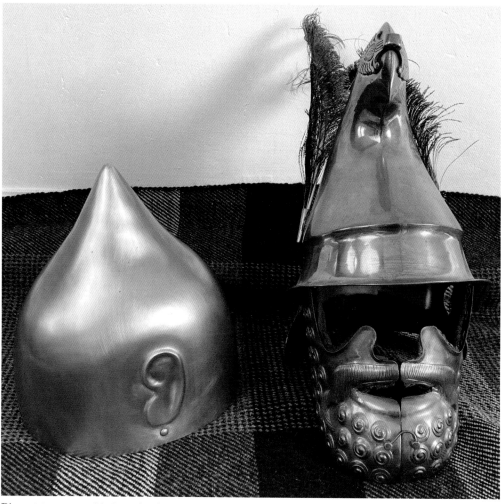

Phoenician pointed helmet (left) and Hellenistic Phrygian helmet (right). (*Photo and copyright by Denis Taverne of Make Carthage Great Again*)

one-quarter of their agricultural production in tribute to Carthage and to provide large numbers of soldiers for their armies. Over time, as mentioned above, from the fusion of some Carthaginian communities with the Libyans the new people of the Liby-Phoenicians emerged. These soon started to play an important role within the Carthaginian military forces, providing the bulk of their foot soldiers. Originally, the Liby-Phoenician infantrymen – like the members of Carthage's citizen militia – were trained and equipped as heavy infantry, fighting in close formation with full armour, but with short spears, more or less like contemporary Greek hoplites. During the early phases of the First Punic War, the Liby-Phoenician infantry was defeated on several occasions by the Romans, who had a great tactical superiority thanks to the flexibility of their legions. As a result of these setbacks, the Carthaginian authorities decided to modernize their Liby-Phoenician contingents under the guidance of a Spartan mercenary military commander named Xanthippus. During 256 and 255 BC, Xanthippus reorganized and redrilled the Liby-Phoenician infantry according to contemporary Hellenistic military tactics, which dominant during this period. The North African soldiers were grouped into a series of phalanxes, each of which consisted of around 4,000 men deployed on the field of battle in 256 files of sixteen heavy infantrymen. They wore bronze or linen cuirasses and were armed with long pikes, in perfect Hellenistic fashion. The 2,500 elite heavy infantry of the Sacred Band were also re-equipped in Macedonian style, with linen armour and long pike. The great victories obtained by Xanthippus over the Romans convinced the Carthaginians that the military model created by Alexander the Great was the best one to adopt. The Liby-Phoenician infantry continued to be organized and equipped as phalangites until the Second Punic War, during which Hannibal decided to modify some of their main tactical features by adopting various Roman elements. In 217 BC, following the Battle of Lake Trasimene, the Liby-Phoenician soldiers replaced their linen cuirasses with the many chainmail that were captured from the defeated Romans, Hannibal wanting to equip his elite heavy infantrymen exactly like the Roman legionaries. At the Battle of Cannae the following year, the Liby-Phoenician infantry consisted of two massive phalanxes with 4,000 men in each, which were equipped with captured Roman armour but still wielded their usual long pikes.

The Carthaginian forces also included the famous war elephants, impressive beasts specifically trained for field combat. During the early decades of Carthage's long history, the Carthaginian Army also had some contingents of war chariots imported from the Middle East, which were apparently soon substituted by the war elephants from northern Africa. These were not what we now know as African Elephants (*Loxodonta africana*), but were a species that is now extinct (*Loxodonta cyclotis*). The elephants used by the Carthaginians were much smaller than those of the contemporary Hellenistic armies, but could be domesticated and trained for use in combat quite easily. They reached a maximum height of 2.5m and had huge ears with rounded lobes. These elephants were taken from the wild in the extensive woodlands that covered the southern part of ancient Algeria and Morocco. They were mostly employed as a psychological weapon, but could easily crush enemy formations with their savage frontal charges. During combat, the Carthaginians placed wooden superstructures protected by shields – known as towers – on the backs of their biggest war elephants, containing one or two soldiers, usually armed with missile weapons. However, most of the Carthaginian war elephants were too small to carry a tower on their backs, only being ridden by their *mahout* or driver. It was known that horses hated the smell of elephants, so the approach of the beasts could cause the breaking up and scattering of enemy cavalry contingents. Consequently, war elephants were frequently employed as an effective anti-cavalry weapon. During battles, however, the pain of the wounds inflicted on the elephants and the volume of battlefield noise could drive them mad, making them equally dangerous to their masters as to their enemies. Following defeat in the Second Punic War, Carthage was deprived of its remaining war elephants by the Romans and was forbidden from taming any others.

The Carthaginian Navy deployed the most formidable warships of Antiquity, which were constructed from pre-cut sections. This innovative method, invented by the Carthaginians, enabled them to mass-produce hulls. The various components of each vessel were marked with distinctive letters in order to speed up their assembly. Most of the Carthaginian warships were heavier than the Greek triremes, consisting of quadriremes and quinqueremes (vessels with four or five rowers moving each oar). Thanks to the excellent training of their crews and the light hulls of their vessels, the Carthaginian warships were more mobile than the early ones of the Romans. Carthaginian naval officers were masters in employing their vessels' deadly rams to sink enemy warships, to do which they could employ many different manoeuvres. Carthage had two impressive harbours: a rectangular one for mercantile vessels and a circular one for its military vessels, which were linked by a channel. In the centre of the military harbour was the Admiral's Island, which was the main base of the Carthaginian Navy and was linked to the shore by a causeway. The circular harbour was enclosed by high stone embankments and the Admiral's Island incorporated roofed sheds for 220 vessels as well as storage magazines for naval equipment. High above the sheds was the house of the admiral commanding the fleet, from which orders could be communicated by the sounding of trumpets. While the military harbour was one of Carthage's most important fortifications, the whole city was located at the head of a roughly hammer-shaped isthmus that was difficult to besiege. The urban centre was protected by a triple wall on the landward side and by a single wall on the seafront. The crews of the Carthaginian warships comprised the poorest inhabitants of the city, who preferred serving as sailors instead of being recruited as soldiers. Naval officers, like those of the army, came from the wealthiest noble families.

Equipment and tactics

All Carthaginian warriors, especially before the Second Punic War, wore their national Phoenician-style long-sleeved tunic, which did not extend below the calves. The tunics of the richest officers were purple and decorated with rich embroidering, which could be golden. The common soldiers mostly wore white tunics, except for

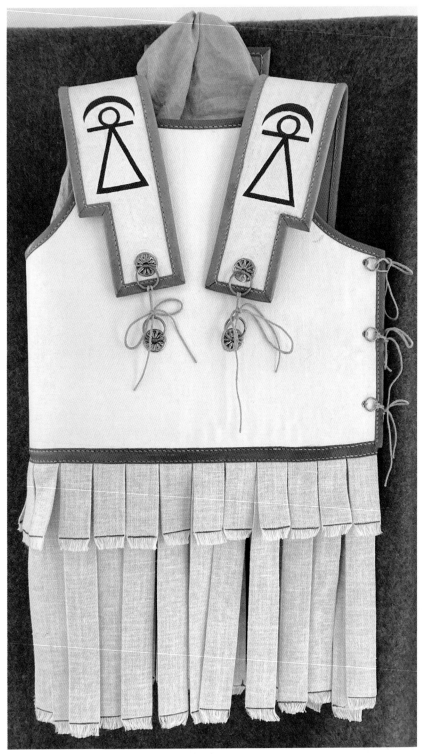

Carthaginian linothorax cuirass. (*Photo and copyright by Denis Taverne of Make Carthage Great Again*)

the youngest warriors who had red tunics to hide bloodstains. After the Second Punic War, shorter tunics of Greek cut became increasingly popular, but these continued to be decorated with traditional Carthaginian symbols such as rosettes, astral elements and floral motifs. Decorative fringes in contrasting colours were usually applied to the external edges of the richest warriors' tunics. Officers were easily distinguished on the battlefield as they wore the skin of wild animals around their head and shoulders, particularly those of lions and leopards. The Liby-Phoenicians, especially before the adoption of those in the shorter Greek style, wore large unbelted tunics. The Carthaginians always wore sandals, while the Liby-Phoenicians often marched barefoot. Nose-rings and the practice of tattooing the cheeks were extremely common, the Liby-Phoenicians also tattooing other parts of their bodies – including their arms and legs – in the usual Berber fashion. Earrings and other jewels were worn by most of the richest warriors. Many Liby-Phoenicians had their hair hanging down in close curls, while Carthaginians had their hair forming a distinctive knot on the top back of the head. Most of the Carthaginians had thick beards, rolled and curled in ringlets according to the traditional Phoenician fashion. The early Carthaginian citizens-soldiers were equipped as heavy infantrymen, similarly to the contemporary Greek hoplites, with bronze helmet (with pointed Assyrian shape or of the Greek Corinthian model), bronze muscle cuirass, bronze greaves, spear, short sword with straight blade and a round shield (a local version of the Greek hoplon). This personal equipment was also used by the Sacred Band. Helmets could sometimes be decorated with horns curving over their wearers' temples, such decoration being linked to the cult of Baal-Hammon, a god with horns. Carthaginian shields, during the early period of the citizens-soldiers but also later, were usually decorated with blazons that had religious meanings: the Apollonian griffin, the Lernian Hydra, the club of Herakles (venerated as the god Melqart in Carthage), the Medusa's head, the Apotropaic Eye, the Sign of Tanit and the Horse of Adad (Tanit and Adad being two of the most important Carthaginian gods).

During the First Punic War, Xanthippus completely re-equipped both the Sacred Band and the Liby-Phoenicians as heavy infantry phalangites. The main offensive weapon of the Carthaginian phalangites was the sarissa pike, an over-long spear measuring 4–6m in length. The sarissa, introduced by the Athenian general, Iphicrates, was perfected by Philip II of Macedonia and completely replaced the traditional hoplite spear (the dory), being superior to the dory in one important aspect: it was 2–3m longer, thereby extending the rows of overlapping spears projecting from the infantry formations towards the enemy and making the infantry phalanxes much stronger than before. The sarissa was made of tough and resilient cornel wood, which was particularly hard but also very heavy; indeed, each pike

Carthaginian hoplon shield painted with the Apotropaic Eye emblem. (*Photo and copyright by Denis Taverne of Make Carthage Great Again*)

weighed approximately 5.5–6.5kg. It had a sharp iron head shaped like a leaf and a bronze butt-spike that could be fixed to the ground when defensive formations were deployed. The spike – made of bronze to protect it from rust – was also very sharp and could easily pierce an enemy shield like the head of the sarissa. An important function of the spike was that it balanced the whole sarissa, making it easier for the infantrymen to wield. It could also be used as a 'back-up' point in case the main head should break during combat.

The sheer bulk and length of the sarissa required the phalangites to use it with both hands, so for protection they carried only a 60cm pelte round shield suspended from the neck to cover their left shoulder. The pelte shield was very small and light, being of use only against enemy arrows; the main defence of the phalangites was the offensive potential of their pikes. It was not easy for a Roman legionary to engage a phalangite in close combat, since he had to get past the wall of enemy pikes before coming into contact with them. Outside the tight formation of the phalanx, however, the sarissa was of little use, as it was very heavy and thus slowed down all the user's movements. During marches, the sarissa, which was composed of two lengths of wood, was carried disconnected on the shoulders. The two sections were only joined by a central bronze tube when needed, a few minutes before the beginning of a battle. Thanks to intensive training, the phalangites learned how to wield their pikes in unison, swinging them vertically to wheel about and then lowering them to the horizontal. The uniform 'swish' produced by this movement of the pikes daunted many enemies and was a useful psychological weapon. The Carthaginian phalangites were deployed in their usual close formation only when they reached the battlefield. Their wall of pikes had five rows of sarissae projecting in front of the first line. The back rows of each phalanx, which could not strike the enemy, held their pikes angled upwards in readiness, and could rapidly fill any gaps in the phalanx opened by enemy arrows or other injuries. The practice of bearing the sarissae of the back rows angled upwards also helped to deflect incoming arrows.

In addition to their pike, the Carthaginian phalangites had two different types of sword, both short and made of iron: the kopis and the xiphos. The kopis was a heavy cutting sword with a forward-curving, single-edged blade. Wielded one-handed, it had a blade length of 48–65cm, which pitched forward towards the point and was concave on the part located nearest to the hilt. The peculiar recurved shape of the kopis made it capable of delivering a blow with the same power as an axe. The xiphos was a one-handed, double-edged short sword with a straight blade measuring 45–60cm. It usually had a midrib and was diamond or lenticular in cross-section. The xiphos had a long point, making it an excellent thrusting weapon specifically designed for close combat.

An important element in the defensive equipment of a phalangite was his body armour. By the time of the First Punic War, one of the most popular kinds of armour was the bronze muscle cuirass, with an external surface sculpted in great detail in order to reproduce the anatomy of the torso. This type of cuirass could be quite short, reaching only the waist, or could be long enough to cover the abdomen. It consisted of two separate bronze plates, which were joined together at the sides and at the shoulders with hinges (half of the hinge was attached to the front plate and the other half to the back plate). There were usually six hinges on each cuirass: two on each side and one for each shoulder. On either side of each hinge was a ring that was used to

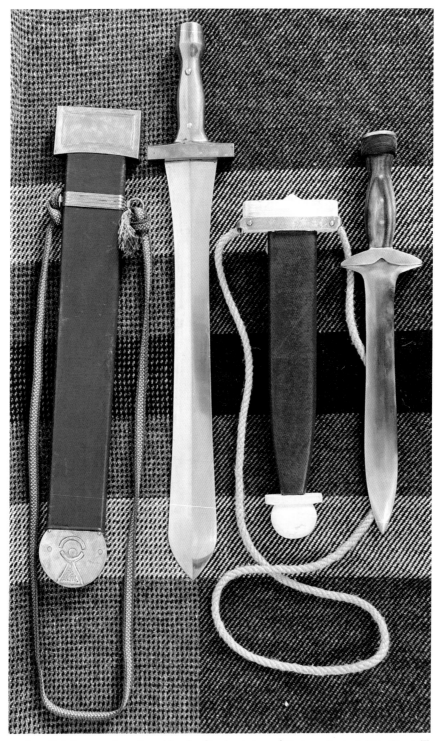

Two examples of *xiphos* sword employed by the Carthaginians. (*Photo and copyright by Denis Taverne of Make Carthage Great Again*)

Carthaginian heavy infantryman bearing *thureos* oval shield, painted with the Sign of Tanit emblem. (*Photo and copyright by Denis Taverne of Make Carthage Great Again*)

pull the two plates of the cuirass together. The muscle cuirass became progressively less popular, to the point that by the beginning of the First Punic War linen had become the standard material for producing corselets. The Carthaginians had started to use linen or leather over previous centuries to produce pteruges, which comprised strips/lappets that were gathered together to form a defensive skirt that could be worn under the bronze cuirass. Extremely effective, especially against enemy arrows, pteruges soon became popular and also started to be used to protect the shoulders and upper arms (being worn under the muscle cuirass on the shoulders).

The linen cuirass was already in use during the First Punic War and had the great advantage of being particularly light and easy to wear. It consisted of multiple layers of linen pressed and glued together to form a corselet about 0.5cm thick. The corselet extended down to the hips and its lower part, below the waist, and had slits to make it easy for the wearer to bend forward. These slits formed a line of pteruges and were part of the main cuirass rather than a separate component of it. Under the main corselet, another layer of pteruges was worn, stuck on the inside of the cuirass to cover the gaps in the pteruges of the outer layer. The whole corselet was produced as a single piece, being wrapped around the torso before being tied together on the left side. A specifically designed U-shaped linen plate was worn on the shoulders, fixed to the back of the corselet and pulled forward to protect the front part of the shoulders. Soon after the appearance of the linen cuirass, an updated version was designed, known as the composite cuirass. Basically, this was a standard linen cuirass that was reinforced by adding bronze scales on its external surface. The scales were usually assembled into a large band around the waist, but they could also be placed on other points of the corselet, such as the shoulders or the loins. Sometimes a linen corselet could be entirely covered with bronze scales, but these costly examples of composite cuirass were quite rare. The body protection of a phalangite was usually completed by a pair of bronze greaves, which covered as far as the knees and were worn with sandals. Greaves could be decorated in many different ways, for example reproducing the anatomy of the lower leg or with geometric patterns. They could be pulled open and clipped on to the leg or strapped on the back. The pelte round shield was made of wicker or wood and was covered with goatskin or sheepskin. It was usually carried with an arm strap with a handle on the rim, but could also be transported on the back, slung on a strap. On the back of the shield was a simple central grip. Generally speaking, the pelte was designed for a fighter who used the sarissa, and was perfectly suited to protect its user from enemy missile weapons.

The defensive equipment of the Carthaginian heavy infantryman was completed by the helmet, which was made of bronze and could have several different shapes. Basically, seven different Hellenistic models of helmet were employed: Corinthian,

Chalcidian, Attic, Phrygian/Thracian, Boeotian, Pilos and Konos. The Corinthian helmet, as implied by its name, was probably designed for the first time in Corinth. It included a frontal plate that covered the entire face, thereby providing excellent protection to the wearer. This frontal plate had three thin slits: two for the eyes and a vertical one for the mouth/nose. On the back, a large curved projection of the helmet protected the nape of the neck. When not fighting, a soldier would wear his Corinthian helmet tipped upward for comfort, releasing most of his face from the frontal plate (which would have assumed an oblique position). One of the main characteristics of the Corinthian helmet was the presence of an indentation in the bottom edge dividing the jawline from the neck, but over the years this was replaced by a simple dart. The greatest fault of the early Corinthian helmets was that they made hearing practically impossible, to ease which the surface of the helmet covering the ears started to be cut away. Before adopting this solution, several experiments were made, leading to the creation of a new helmet that derived directly from the Corinthian model: the Chalcidian helmet. This was lighter and less bulky than the Corinthian helmet, since it left the entire face and ears of the wearer free (there was no frontal plate). In consequence, hearing and vision were much better than the previous type. The Chalcidian helmet consisted of a hemispherical dome under which there were a pair of cheek pieces and a neck guard, while the front had a very small nasal bar. The cheek pieces could be fixed or hinged to the helmet. Adornments of various kinds could be attached to the top of the helmet's dome. Numerous experiments were also made to improve the Chalcidian helmet, and these led to the introduction of a new protective headgear known as the Attic helmet. This was one of the last models of helmet to be developed during the Classical period and thus was widely used during the subsequent Hellenistic period. The Attic helmet was quite similar to the Chalcidian version, but did not have the latter's nose guard. Its cheek pieces were hinged and not fixed, as in later examples of Chalcidian helmet. The Attic helmet soon became extremely popular and over time started to be decorated in a variety of different ways: these included incisions, adornments and protuberances of various kinds that were sculpted or applied on the external surface.

The Phrygian/Thracian, Boeotian and Pilos helmets all derived from soft caps that were worn in the Hellenistic world during daily life. The Phrygian/Thracian helmet started to be produced after the Greeks came into close contact with the warriors inhabiting Thrace and Phrygia, the latter being a region of Anatolia that was populated by a warlike community of Thracian stock who had migrated from Thrace to Asia Minor during the Archaic period of Greek history. As a result, both the Thracians and Phrygians wore the same distinctive soft cap, which had a high and forward-inclined apex. The model of helmet deriving from this cap had this

Carthaginian heavy infantryman wearing Attic helmet and linothorax cuirass. (*Photo and copyright by Denis Taverne of Make Carthage Great Again*)

same apex and was characterized by the presence of a peak at the front that shaded the wearer's eyes and offered some kind of additional protection. Sometimes, instead of the peak, a Phrigyan/Thracian helmet could have a small nasal similar to the one of the Chalcidian helmet. A couple of large cheek pieces were attached to the main part of the helmet; frequently these were large enough to form a facial mask, having only three small gaps for the eyes and nose/mouth. When the cheek pieces were large and joined together to form this mask, the overall appearance of the helmet was not so different from that of the Corinthian version. The Boeotian helmet, as indicated

Two examples of *thureos* shield employed by the Carthaginians. (*Photo and copyright by Denis Taverne of Make Carthage Great Again*)

Carthaginian heavy infantryman wearing pointed helmet and leather cuirass. (*Photo and copyright by Denis Taverne of Make Carthage Great Again*)

by its name, was first developed in the Greek region of Boeotia. Despite being largely used by heavy infantrymen, it eventually became extremely common as a cavalry helmet. In many aspects it was perfect for cavalry use: it was completely open on the face, allowed good peripheral vision and permitted unimpaired hearing. The Boeotian helmet consisted of a domed skull surrounded by a wide, flaring, downward-sloping brim. The brim came down at the rear to protect the back of the neck, but also projected forward over the forehead to work as a sort of visor. On the sides, the brim had a complex shape, with downward-pointing folds that offered some protection to the lateral areas of the face. In essence, the Boeotian helmet was a bronze version of the petasos sun hat, which was widely worn by the famous Thessalian cavalry. This kind of helmet was usually decorated with a falling horsehair plume instead of a crest. The Pilos helmet was a bronze version of the cap of the same name, which was worn by most of the Hellenic peasants during their everyday life, a brimless skullcap made of felt with a simple conical shape. When at war, Hellenic soldiers generally wore their pilos cap under the helmet for added comfort: as a result, a new model of helmet having exactly the same shape of the cap started to be developed. This was very comfortable to wear and easy to produce, to the point that it became the most common model of helmet produced in Greece. The Pilos helmet was quite tall and thus offered good protection for infantrymen against cavalry. It was completely open and thus gave full vision to its wearer, having only a small visor around the opening. The Konos helmet was the last model of helmet developed during the Classical period and saw widespread use during the Hellenistic period. It was a variation of the Pilos helmet but with two main peculiarities: instead of the visor, it had a thin brim protruding from the base and closely fitting around the wearer's head, and also had bronze ear guards that hung to the jawbone. In essence, it was a Pilos helmet with the characteristic brim of a Boeotian helmet.

Chapter 2

The First Punic War

With the defeat of the warrior king Pyrrhus and the Greek colony of Taras in 272 BC, Rome had acquired control over all the continental territory of southern Italy. The Greek cities of the region were all forced to recognize the Romans as their formal protectors and the local Oscan Peoples (the Lucanians and the Bruttii) had to become *socii* (allies) of the Roman Republic. Since Etruria had previously been conquered and the Picentes were already allies of Rome, most of the Italian peninsula was now under Roman control. Only two areas were still independent: northern Italy (inhabited by several Celtic tribes) and the islands of Sicily, Sardinia and Corsica. The first target of the Romans, after conquering Taras in 272 BC, was Sicily, which was the most fertile region of Italy and produced large amounts of top-quality grain. In addition, thanks to its key location in the centre of the Mediterranean, the island could be used as a perfect base for further expansionist campaigns. From a political point of view, Sicily was extremely fragmented: the western part of the island was in the hands of the Carthaginians, who also controlled Sardinia and Corsica, while the central and eastern parts were ruled by Syracuse, which had gradually imposed its dominance over all the other Greek cities of Sicily. As mentioned in the previous chapter, the Carthaginians and Syracusans had almost constantly been at war with each other for many years. Since 289 BC, this difficult political situation had been furtherly complicated by the appearance of a new local 'actor': the Mamertines. These were Italic mercenaries, mostly Oscans, who had been contracted by Syracuse to fight against the Carthaginians. At that time, the Syracusan Army mostly comprised mercenaries, who came from every corner of the Mediterranean; the Mamertines, whose name meant 'sons of Mars', were the most effective and violent of these. When in 289 BC the Syracusan tyrant who had contracted them died, the Mamertines became a problem for the new government of the Sicilian city. The Syracusans disbanded the large mercenary force that had been employed against the Carthaginians and paid off the Mamertines for their services. While marching back to their homeland, however, the Oscan mercenaries decided to remain in Sicily in order to create their own independent settlement on the island. They thus assaulted Messina and conquered it with a surprise attack, thereby becoming the rulers of the strait that separated mainland Italy from Sicily.

The Mamertines soon transformed themselves into pirates and started to attack all the merchant ships passing across the Strait of Messina. This situation was unacceptable for the Syracusans, who tried unsuccessfully to destroy the Mamertines on several occasions. When Pyrrhus went to Sicily during his Italian campaigns, the former mercenaries formed an alliance with the Carthaginians. Although during the following months they were defeated in battle on several occasions by the Epirotes, they were able to retain control of Messina until Pyrrhus was forced to leave Sicily by the revolts of his former allies, notably by the major Greek cities on the island. In the years following the repulse of Pyrrhus, the Mamertines continued to be supported by the Carthaginians and became even stronger. Soon after the departure of the Epirotes, the city of Rhegion also came under control of the former mercenaries. During the war against Pyrrhus, the Romans had garrisoned Rhegion with a legion of allies formed by Campanians. Rhegion was located across from Messina in mainland Italy and thus controlled the other side of the strait. After the Epirotes abandoned Sicily, the Campanian legionaries revolted against Rome and killed their officers, then proclaimed the independence of Rhegion and formed an alliance with their Oscan 'brothers' in Messina. As a result of these events, the Mamertines formed a piratical kingdom that was centred around the Strait of Messina, preying on any shipping they came across. In 270 BC, the Romans decided to intervene and sent an army against Rhegion, which was besieged and reconquered with the help of Syracuse. At this point the Romans could have sent their troops to Sicily to help the Syracusans against the Mamertines of Messina, but since the latter city was located outside mainland Italy, any Roman intervention would have represented a violation of the treaty existing between the Romans and the Carthaginians (which included Sicily in Carthage's sphere of influence).

During the following years, the Syracusans tried to defeat the Mamertines alone, obtaining a clear victory in battle against them in 265 BC. At this point, being on the verge of destruction, the Oscan pirates formally requested Carthaginian military help in order to continue their resistance. The Carthaginians responded by sending a fleet and installing a small garrison in Messina. The Syracusans, being in no position to fight alone against Carthage in a new war, suspended their operations against the Mamertines. However, Rome then decided to intervene in Sicily in order to avoid the Carthaginians gaining complete dominance over the Strait of Messina by 'using' the Mamertine situation. In 264 BC, using as *casus belli* a request for help sent by some Mamertines who were hostile to the Carthaginians, Rome sent an army to take Messina and thus initiated the First Punic War against Carthage. The Romans easily crushed the Mamertines and occupied Messina before the Carthaginians could react. They now controlled both sides of the strategically important strait and

Carthaginian heavy infantryman bearing oval shield. (*Photo and copyright by Denis Taverne of Make Carthage Great Again*)

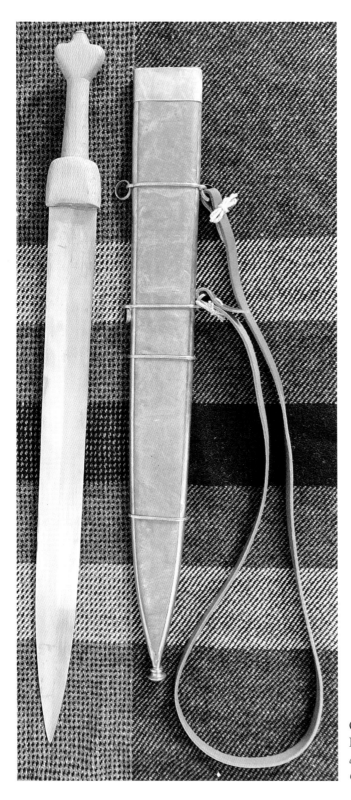

Carthaginian short sword of Iberian fashion. (*Photo and copyright by Denis Taverne of Make Carthage Great Again*)

Carthaginian heavy infantryman equipped with Attic helmet and oval shield; the palm painted on the shield was a very popular emblem among the Carthaginians. (*Photo and copyright by Denis Taverne of Make Carthage Great Again*)

had an important base from which to conquer the rest of Sicily. Fearing that most of their territory could be soon occupied by the Romans, the Syracusans decided to ally themselves with their former Carthaginian enemies. Before the Carthaginians and Syracusans could join their forces, the Romans defeated a Syracusan army and then moved against the Carthaginian force that was marching against Messina. After also defeating the Carthaginians, the Romans secured their control over Messina and then started to besiege Syracuse. On the verge of defeat, Syracuse decided to conclude a truce with the Romans in order to preserve its independence and changed sides in the war. With the resources of their new allies now available, the Romans moved to conquer the central part of Sicily. The Carthaginians assembled most of their forces into the important city of Agrigento, which was besieged for seven months by the Romans before being captured in 261 BC.

By this stage of the war, the Romans had already obtained a series of clear victories on land, but the Carthaginians were still the masters of the Mediterranean Sea. Until that moment, Rome had never had a significant military fleet, being able to deploy a very limited number of small warships. The landing in Sicily had been possible only thanks to the decisive naval support received from the allied Greek cities of southern Italy, which gave the Roman forces in Sicily all the logistic support they needed. If the Romans wanted to defeat the Carthaginians at sea, however, they would need to have their own fleet. Yet achieving this was not a simple matter First of all, building an entire fleet from scratch and in a short time had enormous costs; secondly, the Romans had no experience of naval combat and knew practically nothing of Carthaginian maritime tactics; and finally, the Romans did not possess any naval bases and thus depended on their Greek allies for the construction and repair of their warships. Despite all these problems, the Roman Republic was able to build a fleet of 120 warships in the Greek arsenals of southern Italy and to train 30,000 Italic peasants as sailors in just a few months. The first naval battle between Romans and Carthaginians took place near the Aeolian Islands in 260 BC and ended in defeat for Rome, but after this initial failure the Romans rapidly learned from experience and were able to defeat a Carthaginian fleet at Milazzo. The Roman success here was determined by using the corvus, a new boarding device that was unknown to the Carthaginians, consisting of a mobile wooden bridge with a heavy spike on the underside. By using the corvus, the Romans were easily able to halt and board a Carthaginian warship, thereby effectively transforming a naval clash into a land battle during which the legionaries could employ their superior weapons and tactics as if they were fighting a regular battle. After obtaining their first naval victory, the Romans sent troops to Sardinia and Corsica to expand the conflict to the whole central part of the Mediterranean. In 257 BC, employing a new and larger fleet, the Romans tried to end the war by invading North Africa with an army of 97,000 soldiers. The Carthaginians attempted to prevent the invasion by assembling a fleet of 250 warships with 150,000 men. In the ensuing Battle of Cape Ecnomus, the greatest naval clash of Antiquity, the Romans obtained a decisive victory, destroying most of the enemy vessels. After disembarking in Africa, the Roman expeditionary army obtained some minor victories and threatened to take Carthage, but hostilities were then temporarily suspended to allow peace negotiations to take place, but they produced no positive results.

When the conflict resumed, the Carthaginians reorganized their land forces in Africa and put them under the command of the mercenary Spartan general Xanthippus. He completely transformed the Carthaginian Army, organizing it along Hellenistic lines in a very short time, and was subsequently able to route the Roman army at the Battle of Tunis in 255 BC. The few surviving Roman soldiers were forced to abandon North Africa, but during their journey back to Sicily the entire Roman fleet was destroyed by a terrible storm. In 253 BC, the Romans made another attempt to land troops in Africa, but on this occasion the campaign also ended in failure and the fleet was again destroyed by a storm while returning to Sicily. The situation of the armies in Sicily had not changed much in recent years, with the Romans still controlling the eastern territories and the Carthaginians those in the west. In 249 BC, the rebuilt Roman fleet was destroyed again by Carthaginian forces at the Battle of Trapani. For the following six years, there were no further major clashes on land or at sea, as both Rome and Carthage were exhausted by the lengthy war, having employed all their available resources. By 242 BC, the Romans were finally able to build a new fleet and during the following year they obtained a decisive victory over the Carthaginian navy at the Battle of the Aegates Islands. This marked the end of the First Punic War, Carthage being left in no condition to continue the fight.

Rome obtained very favourable terms from the subsequent peace treaty: the Carthaginians were forced to evacuate Sicily and to pay an immense war indemnity. During the following years, the Carthaginian state went bankrupt due to the financial burden caused by the payment of the reparations, with negative consequences for its empire in the Mediterranean since there was no money left to build new warships or to pay the thousands of mercenaries who made up the Carthaginian Army. The mercenaries then revolted against their masters and ravaged most of present-day Tunisia before being defeated by the Carthaginians. This episode, known as the Revolt of the Mercenaries, had some important consequences for the islands of the Mediterranean. With the Carthaginians temporarily without a fleet and their home city menaced by the mercenaries, the Romans were able to transform Sicily into their first province and also send military expeditions to other islands around the Mediterranean. According

Carthaginian heavy infantryman wearing chainmail cuirass. (*Photo and copyright by Denis Taverne of Make Carthage Great Again*)

to the peace treaty, Sicily was to remain a neutral zone between the possessions of Rome and Carthage, but after the Carthaginians abandoned the island, the Romans occupied most of it except for Syracuse, which was transformed into a Roman protectorate. When the Second Punic War broke out, the city of Syracuse would revolt against the Romans, but it was eventually conquered and annexed to the Roman province of Sicily. The situation in Sardinia and Corsica was somewhat different. The Carthaginian garrisons there, which had not been defeated by the Romans during the course of the First Punic War, were entirely made up of mercenaries. When these fighters were not paid by Carthage at the end of the conflict, they revolted like their comrades in North Africa and devastated many of the towns in which they were garrisoned. Taking advantage of this situation, and presenting itself as the defender of the local Sardinian and Corsican peoples, Rome sent military expeditions to both islands and transformed them into another new province after defeating the revolting mercenaries. By 227 BC, Sardinia and Corsica were both firmly under the control of Rome, despite sporadic rebellions by the local population. During the Second Punic War, the Sardinians revolted against Rome and obtained several military victories, but these last serious attempts of rebellion were ultimately crushed by the Roman legions.

With its victory in the First Punic War, Rome had definitively transformed itself from a regional power into a Mediterranean

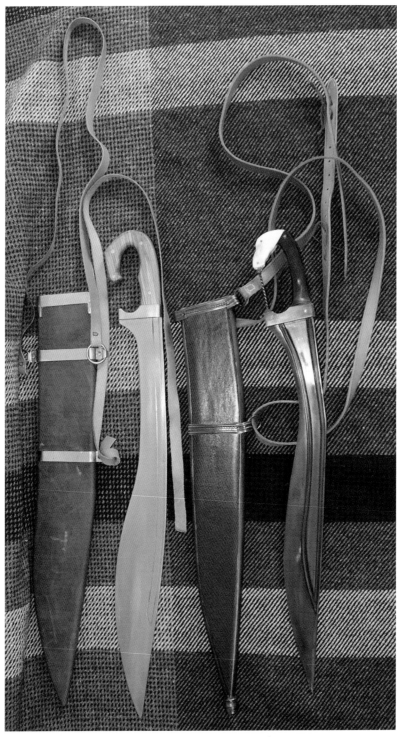

Two examples of *falcata* sword employed by the Carthaginians. (*Photo and copyright by Denis Taverne of Make Carthage Great Again*)

Carthaginian heavy infantryman wearing a chainmail cuirass taken from the Romans. After the Battle of Cannae, the whole Carthaginian heavy infantry was re-equipped with mail cuirasses taken from the Roman legionaries who had been killed. (*Photo and copyright by Denis Taverne of Make Carthage Great Again*)

one. The only part of mainland Italy that was still free from its rule was the vast northern area towards the Alps dominated by the Celtic tribes. In 249 BC, the Celts of Cisalpine Gaul ('Gaul south of the Alps'), being under strong Roman pressure and hoping to take advantage of the ongoing conflict between Rome and Carthage, decided to ask for help against Rome from their 'cousins' of Transalpine Gaul ('Gaul north of the Alps'). The Celts from present-day France, being in search of new lands due to the effects of overpopulation, gave a positive response to this request and sent a large army into northern Italy. According to ancient sources, this comprised some 50,000 foot warriors and 25,000 cavalry. Thanks to these new resources, the Italian Celts were able to resume their hostilities against the Roman Republic. We have no precise details about these 75,000 warriors who marched south into Italy, although ancient writers call them the Gaesatae, using a term that probably meant 'mercenaries' in the Celtic language. This seems to confirm that the Gaesatae were not migrating to Italy with their families and goods, but instead were probably warriors who had been recruited by Cisalpine emissaries. The population of Transalpine Gaul was greatly increasing at this time and there were too few resources to sustain such a large number of inhabitants, so minor warlords and young warriors were in search of new opportunities and new lands because their traditional home territory had little more to offer. The army of 75,000 mercenaries from north of the Alps looked more 'barbarian' to

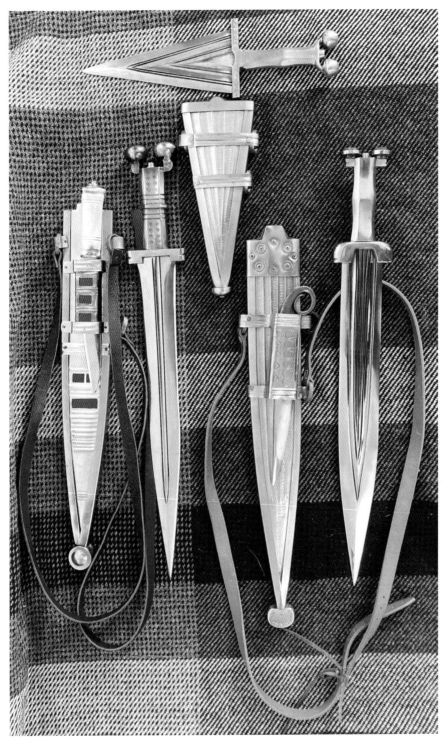

Display of Iberian short swords and daggers employed by the Carthaginians. (*Photo and copyright by Denis Taverne of Make Carthage Great Again*)

the Romans than those tribesmen living in northern Italy, having experienced very little contact with the Mediterranean world and thus preserving their original Celtic identity. The Roman Republic was caught by surprise by the arrival of the warriors from Gaul and initially had serious problems in containing them. Hostilities between the Romans and Gauls lasted for many years, until 225 BC, the Gaesatae proving themselves excellent warriors and defeating the Republic on several occasions. In that year, however, a decisive clash was fought at Telamon between a Roman army and the Celtic forces. The Gallic warriors were badly defeated, suffering enormous losses. The military power of the Gaesatae had finally been broken, but the same could not be said of the spirit of the Cisalpine Gauls. In 223 BC, in an attempt to at long last crush the resistance of the enemy, Rome sent an army of 40,000 soldiers into northern Italy. The Roman offensive proved successful from the beginning, some Celtic tribes deciding to side with Rome in the hope of acquiring new lands. During the following year, another major pitched battle was fought between the Romans and Gauls at Clastidium, where the Cisalpine Celts were utterly defeated and their whole territory in northern Italy was occupied by Rome, including the important centre of Mediolanum (modern Milan). Cisalpine Gaul had finally fallen and the Romans were now the masters of the whole Italian peninsula. However, the Celts had only surrendered because they had no more resources to continue the fight. At the first occasion, they would revolt against Rome in order to regain their freedom. This opportunity came just a few years later in 218 BC, when the Second Punic War broke out between Carthage and Rome.

Chapter 3

The Second Punic War

As we have seen, following the end of the First Punic War, Carthage experienced a serious of internal problems. First of all, there was the massive revolt of the mercenaries who had taken part in the conflict against Rome but had not been paid by the Carthaginians. They revolted against their former employers during what was known as the Mercenary War or Truceless War, which almost caused the destruction of Carthage. The massive military mutiny was eventually crushed by Hamilcar Barca in 237 BC, but the Roman Republic took advantage of the Carthaginian difficulties to annex Sardinia and Corsica. Following these events, Hamilcar became the most important political and military leader of Carthage, being the first to understand that his city needed to find new economic and military resources if it wanted to fight a new war against Rome. These resources could be found only in Iberia, where Carthage already had some important bases. Iberia was full of natural resources that merely needed to be exploited, and was a land of fierce warriors who could be recruited by the Carthaginians as mercenaries or allies. Within about a decade, by conducting numerous harsh campaigns against the Iberian tribes, Hamilcar was able to conquer most of south-eastern Iberia for Carthage. Using his personal charisma and diplomatic intelligence, he transformed the most important local tribes into Carthaginian allies and harshly submitted any communities that resisted his rule. However, Hamilcar died in 229 BC – according to some sources drowning while crossing a river. In 226 BC, as a result of Hamilcar's expansion in Iberia, Carthage and Rome signed the Ebro Treaty, according to which the Ebro River was to mark the border between Carthaginian Iberia and independent Iberia. In 220 BC, however, Rome formed a military alliance with the Iberian city of Saguntum that was situated south of the Ebro. Command of the Carthaginian military forces in Iberia had by now been assumed by Hamilcar's son, Hannibal. Extremely ambitious and audacious, Hannibal decided to attack Saguntum in 219 BC. The city was captured and sacked after a dramatic siege. It appeared that the Carthaginians were in search of a *casus belli* with which to resume hostilities with the Roman Republic, which duly declared war on Carthage in 218 BC, thereby initiating the Second Punic War.

Initial military operations of the war were favourable to the Romans, who repulsed a Carthaginian attack against western Sicily and captured the strategically important

Carthaginian medium
infantryman wearing
Montefortino helmet and
leather cuirass. (*Photo and
copyright by Denis Taverne of
Make Carthage Great Again*)

Carthaginian medium infantryman equipped with falcata sword and *thureos* shield. (*Photo and copyright by Denis Taverne of Make Carthage Great Again*)

island of Malta. Rome was also assembling a large army to be sent to Iberia, but before the expedition could leave Italy there was a major revolt by the Celts of Cisalpine Gaul, a region that had not yet been fully pacified by the Romans. Realizing that the Italian peninsula was vulnerable and that it could be invaded from the north, Hannibal decided to launch an audacious attempt – which had never been tried before – to march with a large army (some sources say as many as 90,000-strong) from southern Iberia to northern Italy by crossing the mountain ranges of both the Pyrenees and the Alps. Rome's control of the Mediterranean with its warships made a seaborne Carthaginian invasion of Italy impossible, so the Romans felt confident that their homeland could never be attacked by the Carthaginians. Against all odds, Hannibal crossed the Pyrenees and entered southern Gaul, where he fought a major battle against the local Celts to cross the Rhone River. The Carthaginians reached the Alps by late autumn, crossed them after surmounting enormous logistical difficulties as well as defeating the resistance of the local Celtic communities. When Hannibal descended from the Alps into northern Italy, he commanded an army that had dwindled to just 26,000 warriors (20,000 infantry and 6,000 cavalry) and a few war elephants. After fighting some more minor clashes against the Celts of Cisalpine Gaul, the Carthaginian warlord formed a strong anti-Roman alliance with them and started moving south. He encountered the first Roman army sent against him at the Battle of the Ticinus, routing it largely thanks to his brilliant cavalry tactics. This victory was very important to Hannibal, as it convinced all the Celts of Italy to join the invading Carthaginians. The Romans tried to stop Hannibal by assembling another large army in northern Italy that had originally been sent to Sicily in view of a planned Roman invasion of North Africa. The unified Roman military forces, however, were crushed by Hannibal at the Battle of the Trebbia, where of the 42,000 Roman soldiers who took part, only some 10,000 were able to escape. Following his second victory in Italy, Hannibal wintered in the north of the peninsula and recruited more Celts, boosting the number of warriors under his command to roughly 60,000.

Following the Battle of the Trebbia, the Romans recruited more legions and formed two new armies to guard the land routes of the western and eastern coastlines connecting northern and central Italy. However, Hannibal outwitted his opponents by crossing the Apennines mountain range in the centre of the peninsula, and was thus able to enter central Italy unopposed in the early spring of 217 BC. The Carthaginians cut off from Rome the largest of the two armies and destroyed it at the Battle of Trasimene, where the Romans were ambushed and suffered enormous casualties (around 15,000 killed and 10,000 captured). After this crushing victory, Hannibal could continue his march south unopposed and entered Apulia in the hope of convincing most of the local Italic and Greek communities to rebel against Rome

Carthaginian light infantryman equipped with pointed helmet and oval shield. (*Photo and copyright by Denis Taverne of Make Carthage Great Again*)

Libyan light infantryman.
(*Photo and copyright by
Denis Taverne of Make
Carthage Great Again*)

and join his cause. After the disaster at Trasimene, the Romans elected as dictator Quintus Fabius Maximus, who adopted a new strategy that included avoiding pitched battles but instead harassing the enemy with guerrilla methods. In 216 BC, however, two new consuls with much more aggressive military plans were elected: Gaius Terentius Varro and Lucius Aemilius Paulus. The pair were authorized by the Senate to raise a massive army of 86,000 men and march against Hannibal in Apulia. Here, however, they were crushed at the Battle of Cannae. During this epic clash, the Roman legions forced their way through the Carthaginians' deliberately weak centre but were then surrounded by the enemy infantry deployed on their flanks. When Hannibal's cavalry attacked the legionaries from the rear after having routed the Roman mounted troops, a massacre of the tightly packed Roman legions unfolded. Around 67,000 Romans were killed or captured in what was the greatest disaster in the military history of Rome.

After the events at Cannae, the peoples of southern Italy changed sides and joined the Carthaginian invaders in the hope that they could free them from Roman dominance. Capua and Taras, two of the richest and largest cities of the region, allied themselves with Hannibal, the former becoming the main base of the Carthaginians in Italy. At this point of the war, however, Hannibal found himself in a difficult situation: he had defeated the Romans on several occasions and had occupied much of Italy, but he was in no position to attack the walled and well-fortified city of Rome. The Carthaginian leader asked for reinforcements on several occasions, but he received only a few thousand soldiers from the government of his city. Carthage was more interested in events that were taking place on other fronts, notably in Iberia, and had no intention of wasting more resources in Italy. Meanwhile, the Roman Republic took drastic steps to raise new legions, which included enrolling the poorest citizens and even slaves. For eleven years after the Battle of Cannae, military operations surged around southern Italy, where the Carthaginians occupied several cities that were soon reconquered by the Romans. It was a period of sieges and counter-sieges, of marches and counter-marches. The Roman Republic was eventually able to field more than 100,000 men against Hannibal, who saw his own forces being consumed in a series of minor and indecisive clashes. By 207 BC, the Carthaginians had been confined to the extreme south of Italy and most of their Italic allies had been defeated by the Romans, including Capua, which was occupied. While these events took place in peninsular Italy, some minor fighting took place in Sicily, where the Carthaginians tried to form an alliance with Syracuse. The city was besieged by the Romans in 213 BC and, despite using innovative war machines designed by the famous inventor Archimedes, was finally taken by the legionaries. The Carthaginians responded by landing an army that occupied several Roman-garrisoned locations in

Sicily, but the invading forces were later crippled by an epidemic and had to reduce their offensive operations. During 211 and 210 BC, the Carthaginian troops in Sicily suffered severe losses and were gradually expelled from their positions. In the spring of 207 BC, Hasdrubal Barca, brother of Hannibal, marched across the Alps with an army of 30,000 men and tried to join forces with the Carthaginian troops in southern Italy. However, Hasdrubal was defeated by the Romans at the Battle of the Metaurus, meaning Hannibal did not receive his long-awaited and badly needed reinforcements. A new Carthaginian army landed in north-western Italy under the command of Mago in 205 BC, its size being rapidly expanded by absorbing large numbers of local Ligurian and Celtic allies. Mago, however, was not able to join forces with Hannibal in southern Italy, and was defeated by the Romans at the Battle of Insubria in 203 BC. Soon after these events, an increasingly isolated Hannibal was forced to leave southern Italy with his battle-hardened veterans, since Publius Cornelius Scipio had invaded Carthaginian North Africa with a large Roman army.

While the events described above were taking place in Italy, the Second Punic War was also being fought on a large scale in Iberia. In 218 BC, a Roman army landed in north-eastern Iberia and obtained an initial victory over the Carthaginians at the Battle of Cissa. This was followed in 217 BC by a naval clash that took place on the Ebro River and was won by the Roman warships. These two Roman successes in Iberia blocked the Carthaginian troops in Iberia south of the Ebro and prevented the despatch of reinforcements to Hannibal in Italy. In 215 BC, Hasdrubal, the overall Carthaginian commander in Iberia, was soundly defeated by the Romans at the Battle of Dertosa, following which many Celtiberian communities, all of whom had been loyal allies of the Carthaginians until that moment, changed sides and joined the Romans. Saguntum was captured in 212 BC by Roman troops, but these were later defeated at the Battle of the Upper Baetis. After this disaster, the Romans were abandoned by the Celtiberians and were forced to fall back to their coastal strongholds located north of the Ebro. In 210 BC, Publius Cornelius Scipio arrived in Iberia with substantial reinforcements and assumed overall command of Roman forces in the theatre. He captured the most important Carthaginian city in Iberia, New Carthage (modern Cartagena), in 209 BC, and started to gain the upper hand in military operations. Hasdrubal and Scipio clashed at the Battle of Baecula in 208 BC, which ended in an indecisive victory for the Romans. Indeed, after this clash, the Carthaginians were able to move north and cross the Pyrenees with the objective of reaching Italy (where Hasdrubal was defeated, as we have seen, at the Battle of the Metaurus). In 206 BC, Scipio crushed the remaining Carthaginian forces in Iberia at the Battle of Ilipa, defeating an army that comprised 54,000 warriors and thirty-two war elephants. During the following year, the Carthaginians, under the command of

Libyan light infantryman equipped with *falcata* sword and small round shield. (*Photo and copyright by Denis Taverne of Make Carthage Great Again*)

Libyan light infantryman equipped with throwing javelin and small round shield. (*Photo and copyright by Denis Taverne of Make Carthage Great Again*)

Mago, tried to recapture New Carthage but were repulsed. After this failed attempt, Mago moved north to cross the Pyrenees and go on to reach Italy (where he was eventually defeated at the Battle of Insubria). Following these events, by 204 BC, the whole of Carthaginian Iberia came under Roman control.

After landing in Africa in 204 BC, Scipio was joined by the Numidians of Masinissa. At that time, the two major kingdoms of the Numidians were fighting each other in a bitter civil war. One of the kingdoms was ruled by Masinissa, who allied himself with the invading Romans, while the other was ruled by Syphax, who remained loyal to Carthage. The Roman support for Masinissa enabled him to rapidly occupy the kingdom of Syphax. In the autumn of 202 BC, after failed peace negotiations, the decisive Battle of Zama took place, finally ending the Second Punic War. Scipio and his Iberian veterans defeated Hannibal and his troops from Italy after several hours of bitter fighting, the clash being decided by the superiority of the Roman cavalry (including a substantial number of Numidians) and the failure of an attack by the Carthaginian war elephants. The victorious Scipio was awarded the name 'Africanus' in recognition for his achievement in finally defeating Hannibal and bringing the war to a successful close. After their victory at Zama, the Romans imposed harsh peace terms on the defeated Carthaginians, who had to renounce all their overseas territories and many of their African possessions. Additionally, the Carthaginians were forbidden from possessing war elephants and from having a fleet of more than ten warships. Finally, they had to pay an immense indemnity of 10,000 silver talents over fifty years and had to send numerous aristocratic hostages to Rome. Carthage thereby lost most of its political autonomy and had to renounce its status as a first-rate Mediterranean power. After the end of the Second Punic War, Masinissa emerged as the most powerful ruler in North Africa, taking advantage of Carthage's military weakness for almost fifty years to enlarge his territorial possessions. Rome backed Masinissa's seizures of and raids into Carthaginian lands until 151 BC, when Carthage was finally able to pay off its war indemnity and to raise a new army.

Chapter 4

The Third Punic War and the Roman Conquest of Iberia

During the five decades that followed the Battle of Zama, the Roman Senate continued to worry about the possibility of a Carthaginian resurgence, especially after the economy of Carthage started to recover. However, the Carthaginians had no intention of fighting a new war against Rome, sending several diplomatic missions to discuss the matter with the Senate, but failed to alter Rome's plans regarding their city. In 149 BC, following the Battle of Oroscopa in which the Carthaginians defeated Masinissa, the Romans seized the port city of Utica in North Africa and declared war on Carthage, this time with the objective of finally destroying the city and all its possessions. The Carthaginians sent diplomatic representatives to Utica before the Romans could invade their lands, hoping that a new peace settlement could be reached, but Rome responded by stating that peace was possible only if the Carthaginians handed over all their weapons. Unprepared for war with Rome, the Carthaginian government accepted these terms and handed all its weapons to the invaders, together with the few warships of its fleet. Nevertheless, once Carthage was fully disarmed, the Romans made further demands: the Carthaginians were asked to abandon their city and to relocate it 10 miles inland from the sea. At this point the Carthaginian representatives abandoned the negotiations and the city started preparing for a long siege. Carthage was well fortified, protected by massive walls, so it would not be easy for the Romans to mount a successful siege. Indeed, two frontal assaults conducted by the Romans were repulsed during the opening phase of the siege, while the Carthaginians harassed their enemy's supply lines and foraging parties with lightning-fast raids. Carthaginian troops, led by an experienced commander named Hasdrubal, attacked the Roman camps located outside the city on several occasions and obtained a series of minor victories. In 148 BC, Roman operations quietened down and the siege became a looser blockade, the Carthaginians launching further attacks against the Roman positions.

In 147 BC Scipio Aemilianus, whose adoptive grandfather was Scipio Africanus, was elected consul in Rome and was appointed as overall commander of the legions in Africa. The change of leadership had immediate positive consequences for the Romans, Scipio organizing a successful night attack against Carthage and breaking into the city with a token force of 4,000 men. After having destroyed the suburbs of the capital, however, the Romans returned to their camps as they were too few to resist a Carthaginian counter-attack. At this point of the war, Scipio built an immense mole to cut off access to the harbour of Carthage, in an attempt to force his enemies into starvation, but the Carthaginians responded by cutting a new channel that connected the harbour to the sea. The Carthaginians were even able to build a new fleet and to attack the Roman ships during what became known as the Battle of the Port of Carthage. However, the Carthaginian fleet was decisively defeated. During the following weeks, the Romans gained control of the port's quay and constructed a brick structure as high as the enemy walls, from which up to 4,000 soldiers could fire onto the Carthaginian ramparts from short range. In the last weeks of 147 BC, Scipio attacked the main camp of the Carthaginian troops from several directions and overran it, inflicting serious losses. In the spring of 146 BC, the Romans launched a full-scale assault from the harbour area that finally breached the walls of Carthage. For six days, the legionaries systematically worked their way through the residential areas of the city, killing everyone they encountered and setting ablaze all the buildings. The siege having been a long and bloody affair, the Romans resolved to raze Carthage to the ground. At the end of the massacre, during which thousands of civilians were killed, only 50,000 Carthaginians were left alive; these were all sold into slavery. Meanwhile, the legionaries were said to have sowed the recently destroyed city with salt – a traditional ritualistic act indicating that nothing could grow there again – and pillaged all its treasures. The Punic Wars had finally come to an end, with the ascendancy of Rome as the dominant military power of the Mediterranean world.

During the Second Punic War, realizing that Carthage's power was based on the resources of Iberia, the Romans sent various generals and armies to Spain in order to expel the Carthaginians from the area. After several bloody battles, by the end of the conflict the Romans were able to conquer and occupy all the Iberian lands that had been under Carthaginian control. The local tribes, however, continued to revolt against the Republic for many decades. As we have seen, Punic control had not been particularly strict, but Roman rule was completely different. During these rebellions, the Iberians were helped by the Celtiberians of western Spain, who had remained independent from both Carthage and Rome. Rome quickly understood that the only way to pacify Spain was to also conquer the Celtiberian territories. This, however, proved to be extremely difficult to carry out, the Celtiberians being masters of guerrilla warfare and having intimate knowledge of the mountain territory in which to carry out such tactics. The first Roman moves against the Celtiberians started as early as 197 BC, just a few years after the end of the Second Punic War. From the beginning, the military operations in Spain were characterized by a series

Round shields employed by the Libyan light infantry. (*Photo and copyright by Denis Taverne of Make Carthage Great Again*)

of crushing defeats for the Romans. In 181 BC, the first of two Celtiberian Wars broke out in Spain, ending in 179 BC, when Tiberius Gracchus signed peace treaties with most of the Celtiberian leaders. The Romans had been unable to permanently occupy Celtiberian lands, and thus the peace terms were quite favourable for the Celts, who retained complete control over their lands but in exchange had to provide allied military contingents and amounts of grain for Rome. After more than two decades of relative peace in Iberia, the Second Celtiberian War erupted in 154 BC. This conflict lasted for two years and involved another series of major Celtiberian victories. In order to prevail, the Romans had to use very harsh methods, fighting with great violence and committing a series of abuses against the civilian population.

Carthaginian heavy cavalryman; the members of the elite Sacred Band were equipped similarly to this soldier. (*Photo and copyright by Denis Taverne of Make Carthage Great Again*)

Carthaginian marine wearing heavy personal equipment. (*Photo and copyright by Denis Taverne of Make Carthage Great Again*)

Carthaginian marine wearing light personal equipment. (*Photo and copyright by Denis Taverne of Make Carthage Great Again*)

By 151 BC, it seemed that Rome had finally defeated the Celtiberians, albeit they were still in control of most of their lands. Since 155 BC, however, the Iberian tribes of southern Spain had launched a general revolt against the Romans. The uprising was guided by their great military leader Viriathus and became known as the Lusitanian War (from the name of Viriathus' tribe, the main driving force of the rebellion). In 144 BC, the Celtiberians decided to break their pacts with Rome and join with Viriathus in his revolt. Most of the Iberian and Celtiberian tribes were thus, for the first time, united in pursuit of a common objective – Viriathus dream of expelling the Romans from all the Iberian territories. The war lasted for more than fifteen years until 139 BC. During that time, the Romans were on the verge of losing Spain on several occasions, but in the end Viriathus was assassinated by some of his own men and the rebels were crushed. After these events, Iberia became Roman Hispania and the Republic's dominance over most of present-day Spain and Portugal became much more stable. Most of the Celtiberian lands were occupied, with the exception of some small territories in north-western Spain; here, in present-day Cantabria and Asturias, two tribes continued to resist by using irregular warfare tactics. The area was extremely marginal from an economic point of view, being entirely covered with mountains and located on the western edge of the Roman territories. Consequently, the Cantabri and the Astures were able to retain their independence until the reign of Rome's first emperor, Augustus, more than a century later.

Chapter 5

The Numidians

History and organization

The Carthaginian Army comprised several lightly armed tribal contingents recruited from various areas of northern Africa. They included numerous minor tribes but belonged to five main populations: the Numidians, Mauri, Libyans, Garamantians and Gaetulians. The Numidians were the most important of them, and there is consequently a large amount of information on their military forces, but of the other four peoples we know very little. The Mauri (or Moors) were a Berber population living in an area known as Mauretania from the name of its inhabitants (corresponding to present-day northern Morocco and north-western Algeria). The Libyans were a Berber population like the Mauri and lived in a vast region that extended from the eastern border of Egypt to the western border of Tunisia, between Ptolemaic Egypt and Carthaginian lands during the period of the Punic Wars. The Garamantians and Gaetulians, differently from the Mauri and Libyans who mostly inhabited the Mediterranean coast, were settled in the interior areas of North Africa that were partly covered by the Sahara Desert. It is important to remember that during Antiquity, the coastline of northern Africa was a flourishing agricultural area where vegetation was extremely varied and where large amounts of grain were produced. The Sahara Desert was much smaller than now, and thus in the coastal regions of North Africa it was possible to find several species of animals that are now extinct – such as the small 'Elephant of the Atlas' employed in war by the Carthaginians. The Garamantians were nomads of Berber stock who lived in the interior regions of Libya, on the edges of the Sahara. The Gaetulians, like the Garamantians, were nomads of Berber stock, inhabiting the portion of the Sahara Desert that extended south of the Mauri's lands (from the Atlantic coastline of Morocco to north-western Algeria). The Numidians were also part of the Berbers, the latter term originally being used by the Greeks to indicate all the native inhabitants of northern Africa who spoke languages that had several common features. All the Berber populations were extremely warlike and were used to harsh living conditions, their warriors being lightly armed and used to travelling long distances in arid regions. All the Berber populations allied with Carthage had their warriors equipped as light infantry or light cavalry. The Numidians always had a special relationship with the Carthaginians, inhabiting the interior areas of Tunisia as well as the eastern coastline of Algeria. Differently from the Mauri and the Libyans, the Numidians were also settled in some interior regions, not only along the coast. They were divided into two major tribal groups: the Massyli and the Masaesyli. The Massyli controlled western Numidia and bordered with Carthaginian territory, while the Masaesyli were settled in eastern Numidia, bordering with the Libyans. The Mauri, Libyans, Garamantians and Gaetulians all had many characteristics in common with the Numidians, and thus, by describing the military of the latter, we will also describe the military of these other Berber peoples. It is important to understand, however, that while in Numidian armies light cavalry was more important and numerous than light infantry, in the armies of the other Berber peoples the opposite was the case. The Numidian light cavalry were among the most well-known horsemen of Antiquity, riding barefoot without saddles or bridles in the traditional Berber way and being armed only with a few light javelins. During the Punic Wars, they became well known for their surprise attacks, swift feint retreats and excellent skirmishing abilities. Riding on small but sturdy ponies, they had a great degree of mobility and made up the light cavalry of the Carthaginian armies. Under Hannibal's command, the Numidian horsemen proved their valour on several occasions, defeating larger contingents of Roman cavalry that carried heavy equipment. As we will see in this chapter, however, mounted troops were not the only component of the Numidian armed forces.

By the outbreak of the Second Punic War in 218 BC, the Massyli were ruled by their king, Gaia, and had their capital at Cirta (modern-day Constantine in Algeria), whereas the Masaesyli were ruled by King Syphax and had their capital at Siga (not far from modern-day Oran in Algeria). During the early years of the Second Punic War, both the Massyli and the Masaesyli supported Carthage as loyal allies, sending their best men to fight against the Romans in the Italian peninsula and in Iberia. In 206 BC, however, Gaia died and a civil war broke out within his kingdom to determine the identity of his successor. On one side there was his son, Masinissa, who had already fought for several years against the Romans in Iberia, while on the other there were other relatives of Gaia who wanted to usurp Masinissa's throne. After several bloody clashes, Masinissa was able to secure control of his father's kingdom, but he soon had to face a massive invasion organized by Syphax. Masinissa was defeated and obliged to flee to the interior mountains of his realm, where he continued resisting at the head of a few horsemen by using hit-and-run guerrilla tactics. When Scipio landed in North Africa, Masinissa allied himself with the Romans, and with their decisive support he crushed his rival Syphax at the Battle of

Numidian noble warrior; his tunic is made from the skin of a giraffe, while the sword with annexed knife is of Iberian design. (*Photo and copyright by Denis Taverne of Make Carthage Great Again*)

Cirta in 203 BC. Masinissa thereafter not only reconquered his own realm but also occupied most of Syphax's kingdom, thereby unifying the Numidian communities for the first time in their history. Transforming the Numidians into their main African allies now proved a decisive factor for the Romans, helping to finally determine their success in the Second Punic War. At Zama, Masinissa guided a large contingent of Numidian light cavalry that played a crucial role in the Roman victory. After the end of the Second Punic War, the kingdom of Numidia remained Rome's most powerful and loyal ally in northern Africa, acting as a guardian of Roman interests in the regions. The Numidians were tasked with clamping down on any attempted resurgence that could be organized by the defeated Carthaginians. During the Third Punic War, the Numidians – guided initially by the elderly Masinissa and later by his son, Micipsa – once again fought on the Romans' side and helped in their long siege of Carthage. Under Masinissa and Micipsa, the kingdom of Numidia flourished, its economy continuing to be based on semi-nomadic pastoralism but settled agriculture also increasing. New towns were built and large amounts of locally produced grain started to be supplied to the Roman Army.

From the time of the Second Punic War onwards, the Numidian light cavalry functioned as the primary resource of the kingdom, the provision of excellent horsemen to both the Carthaginians and then the Romans gaining the Numidian monarchs increasing prestige. Numidian men learned to ride as young boys and spent much of their early life on horseback, improving their equestrian skills and learning how to hunt by throwing javelins. The Numidian horses were held with a single rein attached to a simple collar, which was made from woven vegetable fibre or hair and worn around their neck. The mounts were guided by touches from a slender wooden rod. The Numidian horses were quite small, but fast and sturdy. While not beautiful animals to look at, their hardiness and stamina made them perfect for military employment. They ate only grass and needed to drink only rarely, meaning they could campaign in the harshest of conditions and maintaining them was not particularly costly. The Numidian horses were never washed or groomed, their hooves were never cleaned and their manes or tails were usually left unbrushed. According to descriptions made by the first-century BC Roman historian Livy, they trotted with their heads stretched out and their necks stiff. Nevertheless, these ungraceful mounts were perfectly suited to the combat tactics employed by their riders, which consisted of repeated short attacks followed by swift feigned retreats. At the Battle of the Trebbia in 218 BC, hundreds of Roman cavalrymen became victims of the Numidians' peculiar way of fighting. Until the outbreak of the Second Punic War, Numidian armies consisted almost entirely of light cavalrymen. In 213 BC, however, Syphax asked the Romans to help him in organizing some well-trained

Numidian light cavalryman equipped with throwing javelins and small round shield. (*Photo and copyright by Denis Taverne of Make Carthage Great Again*)

infantry for his armies. The Roman Republic sent an experienced centurion named Quintus Statorius to the king of the Masaesyli, teaching the Numidian warriors how to deploy in close formation on the battlefield and giving them some basic legionary-style instruction. After Syphax's success in developing a small but effective infantry force, the Numidian armies always included a number of foot warriors. However, they retained their usual light equipment, wearing no helmets and no armour. The Numidian infantryman was basically a light skirmisher, armed with throwing javelins and defending himself only with a small oval shield. Their tactics mirrored those of cavalry, being mostly based on mobility. Over time, the Numidian light cavalry and light infantry started to operate together in a very effective manner, with the foot soldiers beginning to support the mounted warriors by being interspersed among their ranks. The Numidian light infantry included small numbers of archers and slingers, but these were undoubtedly a secondary component of Numidian armies. Numidians also employed war elephants, following the Carthaginian example; these were of the so-called 'forest species', known as *Loxodonta cyclotis*. They were much smaller than the more common African elephants, with more rounded ears and more slender tusks. Numidian war elephants carried only their *mahout*, being equipped with no turrets. There was no need for them to carry armed men on their back, since their bulk was a most effective psychological weapon. Controlling a war elephant on the battlefield was extremely difficult, as the beasts were prone to panicking and could sometimes charge against the soldiers of their own army, meaning the experience of the *mahouts* was decisive in determining their effective employment.

Equipment and tactics

The Numidians, like all the other Berbers, were olive-skinned with dark brown or black hair that could be straight, wavy or curly. They took particular care over their hair, which was often braided or dressed in elaborate styles – it could be shaped to resemble an inverted crescent or twisted into rows or waves. Beards were often long and trimmed into a sharp point, which jutted outward from the chin. The Numidian warriors were small, like their horses, and were well known for their endurance, being able to survive on meagre rations for long periods of time. Numidian clothing was mostly obtained from animal skins or could consist of simple unbelted tunics decorated along the borders. Most of the tunics were white, knee-length and sleeveless. Only those worn by the most prominent individuals were decorated with fringes. The tunics were gathered around the waist by a thin cord and were mostly made of wool, but it was not uncommon to find some made of leather. Thigh-length cloaks, always made of wool, were worn during cold months. Common warriors had no footwear, while those rich enough wore comfortable leather boots.

The main offensive weapon of both the Numidian light cavalry and light infantry was the throwing javelin, which had a leaf-shaped head that was 30cm long and 4cm at its widest point. The metal head had a narrow and circular socket at the

Numidian light infantryman equipped with throwing javelins and small round shield. (*Photo and copyright by Denis Taverne of Make Carthage Great Again*)

base for the attachment of a wooden shaft, which was around 1m long. The Numidian javelin was primarily designed for throwing from short distances, but could also be employed for stabbing during hand-to-hand fighting. Its shaft was quite slender, since it was common for a Numidian warrior to simultaneously grasp three javelins and the grip of the shield in the same hand. Javelins were also employed for hunting and thus were the traditional national weapon of the Numidians, who were admired by both their allies and opponents for their mastery in hitting targets from medium distances while galloping at full speed. Numidian shields could be of two different types: circular or oval. Circular shields were the standard model employed by mounted troops. In most cases these were made of elephant hide, which was up to 2.5cm thick and thus was perfect for producing very tough leather. The external frame of the shield was made from wicker, which was woven into a circle that was rigid enough to hold the thick sheets of elephant hide in the correct shape. On their back, the round shields had a simple hand grip in the centre, made of woven material or wood. Sometimes they could have two attachments – one for the forearm and one for the hand. In most cases, the flat external surface of the shields was not painted, but sometimes it could have coloured decorations. The oval shields employed by the Numidian infantrymen were copied from those used by the contemporary Mediterranean armies, and thus had the same main features.

The Libyan warriors had their heads shaved except for a central plaited crest of hair, which had a crescent-shaped amulet fastened on the front and hanging on the brow. The Garamantian light infantrymen ornamented their long curly hair with gold clasps and painted their bodies with different decorative patterns, like several other Berber warriors.

The Gaetulian light horsemen rode without reins but had saddle-cloths made of coarse linen. The Numidians' fast horses and great horsemanship gave them a great degree of mobility: they could come very close to their opponents in order to throw their javelins from short distances and then withdraw very quickly in order to avoid hand-to-hand engagements. Helmets and armour were not worn, since they would limit mobility; the speed of the Numidian ponies was the best defensive weapon that their riders had, in addition to a simple round shield.

The Numidian tactics developed as a result of the low-intensity warfare that traditionally took place between the various Berber communities of North Africa. The Numidians were not employed to cause severe losses to their enemies, since this was not their main tactical function, but they were perfect for harassing and disrupting enemy formations as well as for luring opponents out of their positions to a place where the Numidians could organize an effective ambush. Thanks to their elusive tactics, the Numidian horsemen generally suffered very few casualties. The Numidian light cavalrymen in Carthaginian service were also employed as mounted scouts, ranging far ahead of the main columns to carry out reconnaissance or to conduct foraging operations and raids.

Chapter 6

The Iberians

History and organization

To the ancient Greeks, Iberia designated the whole territory of present-day Spain and Portugal, which by the beginning of the Punic Wars was populated by several different peoples belonging to two main groups: the Iberians and the Celtiberians. The Iberians were the original Indo-European inhabitants of the Iberian peninsula, who had developed a quite complex civilization during the previous centuries. Since the seventh century BC, the Iberians had been in contact with the Phoenicians and the Greeks, who established colonies on the eastern coastline of Spain, and thus the native population started to assimilate some cultural elements brought from abroad. Rich in agriculture and cattle, the lands inhabited by the Iberians were flourishing economically, having significant natural resources and being perfect for developing trade. By the beginning of the Punic Wars, the southern communities of the Iberians had already built more than 200 urban centres, another element confirming the high degree of development achieved by the inhabitants. Iberia became a land of opportunities for the Phoenician and Greek colonies, since it already had a thriving fishing industry based on the coastal areas and many large mines producing various kinds of precious metals. The benign climate of Iberia favoured any kind of activity connected with agriculture and livestock breeding.

The Iberians were divided into several tribal groups, the most important of which were the Turdetani, Edetani, Ilergetes and Contestani. Each community had its own king and a blood aristocracy, whose prominence depended upon their wealth. The majority of the Iberians were free men, but there was also a working class of semi-slaves – both in public and private employment – as well as a number of outright slaves, captured enemies who were obliged to work for the aristocrats of the various tribal communities. Inter-tribal warfare was extremely common in ancient Iberia, and it was typical for each group to transform the enemies captured during a raid into slaves. The Celtiberians were Iberians who had been progressively 'Celticized', northern and central Iberia having seen the arrival of massive Celtic migratory waves from France during the early Iron Age. The assimilation of the warlike newcomers with the Iberians had created a new people – the Celtiberians – consisting of several

Iberian warrior with padded cuirass.
(*Photo and copyright by Terra Carpetana*)

Iberian warrior armed with spear and sword. (*Photo and copyright by Terra Carpetana*)

Celtiberian warrior bearing oval shield. (*Photo and copyright by Terra Carpetana*)

different tribal groups. The Celtiberians living in north-western Iberia belonged to three main groups: the Gallaeci, Cantabri and Astures. These were more Celtic in nature than the other Celtiberians to the south of their territories and developed a hilltop culture that was similar to that of contemporary Gaul. The geographical isolation of these communities, who lived on a territory covered with mountains and woods, helped preserve most of their distinct Celtic features. The Celtiberians inhabiting the central areas of present-day Spain and Portugal retained several characteristics of the 'pure' Iberians but had the same warlike nature as the northern Celtiberians. Their most important tribal groups included the Lusitani, Vettones, Vaccei, Carpetani, Arevaci and Pellendones. Each of these occupied a whole region of Iberia, based upon a single urban centre that acted as a tribal capital. These capitals were, in most cases, built on top of a hill to be easily defensible and had access to natural water resources within a short distance. Like several of the Iberian cities, these centres of the Celtiberians were surrounded by stone walls and by larger walled perimeters that were intended to offer secure refuge to the population from the countryside in case of emergency. Among the various groups, the Arevaci were the only ones to maintain a nomadic way of life, being a sheep-herding people. The social organization of the Celtiberians was similar to that of the Iberians, comprising a blood aristocracy as well as slaves. In time of peace, each community was guided by a council of elders, but a single military leader was appointed upon the outbreak of war. Iberia was one of the richest regions of the Mediterranean world during Antiquity, with the civilization of the Iberians and Celtiberians being in no way inferior compared with that of the Greeks or the Carthaginians. Indeed, from an economic point of view, Iberia was much richer than the Italian peninsula dominated by Rome.

Broadly speaking, Iberian and Celtiberian societies were organized into basic units called *gentilitates* and *gens* by the Romans; the former being the equivalent of Celtic clans while the latter were similar to Celtic tribes. The smaller clans were united by common blood and by a common founder, their members performing common religious practices and having rights over some collective properties. The various clans or family groups were linked by a series of shared interests, with some clans forming a tribal community, which could be quite large. Frequently, especially in the event of war, several tribal communities joined their forces by forming a larger military alliance or federation of peoples. All the adult males of an urban centre or a village made up a popular assembly that took decisions on matters of collective importance. A restricted assembly of the elders, however, exerted political authority in a much more effective way. Inside each clan, some familiar groups – consisting of a man and his close relatives – were sworn to the service of a prominent individual in

Celtiberian warrior armed with *soliferrum* javelin. (*Photo and copyright by Terra Carpetana*)

Iberian warrior bearing round shield. (*Photo and copyright by Terra Carpetana*)

Iberian warrior armed with sword. (*Photo and copyright by Terra Carpetana*)

return for certain obligations taken on by that individual. This bond existing between an aristocrat and a familiar group had a deep religious significance and a solemn nature. Each clan leader had his own personal bodyguard made up of warriors who had dedicated their life to his service. Inter-clan bonds also existed, with a member of one clan permitted to enjoy full rights and duties as a member of another group. The existence of common properties within the territory of each clan prevented large numbers of individuals falling into poverty and enabled the clan leaders to count on the absolute loyalty of their followers.

Iberian warfare consisted of rapid incursions and brief campaigns conducted on a tribal level, inter-tribal conflicts being extremely frequent. Pillaging and raiding were considered honourable activities by most Iberian men, who treated fighting as an essential component of their daily life. According to the first-century BC Greek historian Diodorus Siculus, the young Iberian males – upon reaching adulthood – went into the mountains of their territory, where they formed large armed bands, which travelled across Iberia for several months at a time gathering riches through robbery before returning to their homelands. This practice – which marked the reaching of adulthood – was not determined by need but by custom, the Iberians believing that a 'true' man could only be respected by his community if he had shown valour in combat away from his home territory. Each able-bodied Iberian male was a potential warrior and was used to very harsh living conditions. Through moving in the mountains of modern-day Spain and Portugal, the Iberian warriors developed their own distinctive way of guerrilla warfare, consisting of hit-and-run tactics based on mobility, and did not favour engagement in large, pitched battles. The Iberians enjoyed gymnastic exercises and frequently organized 'friendly' combat to improve their fighting capabilities. Horsemanship and hunting were also fundamental elements of an Iberian man's daily life, with hunting helping them to practice guerrilla-style movements as well as how to organize ambushes. The horse enjoyed great importance in the social activities of the Iberians, being honoured as a divinity in many sanctuaries. Ancient Spain and Portugal were rich in wild horses, described in some contemporary Roman texts as being extremely fast and particularly beautiful. The great endurance and small dimensions of the Iberian horses made them perfect for military use. Indeed, Iberian contingents fighting during the Punic Wars as part of the Carthaginian armies always included sizeable numbers of cavalry. The Iberians, who were the inventors of the horseshoe and developed an innovative form of riding equipment, were considered among the peoples of the Mediterranean to be unrivalled in horsemanship. They paid special attention to the training of their mounts: one of the most common exercises was to teach the horse to kneel down and remain silent for long periods, which was of great use when Iberian cavalry organized ambushes or had to escape from a numerically superior enemy. Hannibal was an enthusiastic supporter of Iberian cavalry and always tried to have large contingents of Iberian horsemen in his military forces. Differently from the light Numidian horsemen, the Iberians could be employed as heavy shock cavalry to conduct charges.

Equipment and tactics

The common Iberian and Celtiberian warriors were equipped as infantrymen, with either heavier or lighter equipment. The panoply of the heavy foot soldiers comprised armour and an oval shield, while that of the light foot soldiers included only the small round shield known as the *caetra*. In addition to the regular infantry there were the elite slingers from the Balearic Islands. The cavalry comprised those who made up the personal bodyguards of the various clan leaders. These mounted troops were semi-professional soldiers, spending most of their life serving the orders of a warlord. Most of them were bonded to their leader by a religious vow and were thus noted for their loyalty. Some of the Iberian and Celtiberian horsemen were equipped with armour and acted as heavy cavalrymen, while others without cuirasses were mostly employed as mounted skirmishers. Whatever their type, all Iberian and Celtiberian horsemen carried the *caetra* shield, which was originally used by most of the warriors from Iberia until the larger oval shield was brought south of the Pyrenees by the migrating Celts. Light infantrymen, as an alternative to the *caetra*, could also carry a larger model of round shield that offered more protection during close combat. Iberian and Celtiberian military contingents had a tribal internal organization, similar to that of the Celts, with coordination on the battlefield achieved through the use of specific musical instruments, such as horns and trumpets, which were used to transmit orders. Tribal standards were also employed to differentiate the various contingents.

The excellent quality of the Iberian and Celtiberian warriors was one of the main reasons behind the Carthaginians' decision to invade Iberia, as Carthage needed veteran soldiers who could be employed in large numbers against the Romans. Carthaginian penetration into Iberia was not easy, as the local communities resented foreign rule and repulsed any attempt from Carthage to establish a permanent presence on Iberian soil. By using diplomacy more than war, however, the Carthaginians were finally able to establish alliances with most of the Iberian and Celtiberian tribes. Hannibal – like his father Hamilcar, who had spent most of his life fighting in Iberia – realized that most of the Iberian and Celtiberian warriors were interested in fighting as mercenaries for Carthage. Consequently, he did not try to submit the peoples of Iberia by conquering them but preferred to transform them into loyal allies, so they provided large contingents of mercenaries and auxiliaries when needed and permitted

Iberian warrior wearing bronze helmet.
(*Photo and copyright by Terra Carpetana*)

to the Carthaginians to exploit the great natural resources of their homeland. As a result of this strategy, the Iberian and Celtiberian warriors soon became one of the most important components of the Carthaginian Army. The Carthaginian commanders appreciated their courage as well as their resilience, but what was of great use for military leaders like Hannibal was the tactical flexibility of the Iberian and Celtiberian fighters, with contingents that could be equipped to fight as heavy or light infantry and cavalry according to the circumstances. Hannibal tried to re-equip all his Iberian and Celtiberian soldiers – except for the Balearic slingers – with heavy personal armour and weapons since he considered them as his most reliable warriors. After the Battle of Cannae, the thousands of chainmail taken from the massacred Roman troops were used by the Carthaginians to re-equip all their Iberian foot soldiers as heavy infantrymen comparable to the Roman legionaries. Iberian and Celtiberian cavalry fought in loose and very manoeuvrable formations, which could be employed to perform a variety of tactical duties, since they comprised both lightly and heavily equipped horsemen. The light cavalry were perfect skirmishers, equipped with javelins, who could scout in front of their army or clash with enemy mounted troops from a distance. The heavy cavalry, meanwhile, acted as shock troops thanks to their helmets and cuirasses, being capable of

Iberian swordsman. (*Photo and copyright by Terra Carpetana*)

launching effective frontal charges. When needed, all the Iberian and Celtiberian horsemen were trained to dismount and fight on foot. Sometimes they could even employ a peculiar defensive formation, consisting of a ring with the horses placed in the centre. The mounts of the Iberian and Celtiberian warriors had a picket pin attached to their reins, which allowed the rider to tether them in battle.

The Iberian warriors employed several different types of helmets, which could be made of bronze or leather. The most common model had a bascinet-like close-fitting shape and was extremely simple, leaving the face of its wearer completely uncovered. It could have reinforcement bands around its edges – with raised rivets – and be ornamented with a crest, which was usually present on the helmets of noble warriors. The decorative crests of the Iberian warriors could have different shapes, but in most cases consisted of toothed crests or combs. They could even have the shape of sacred

Celtiberian spearman. (*Photo and copyright by Terra Carpetana*)

animals. Occasionally, either one or three sweeping crests made of bronze could be applied on the helmets used by warlords. Simple leather helmets, resembling a cap in their shape, were worn by the majority of the warriors, but even these could sometimes have toothed crests or combs. According to ancient sources, this simple model of cap helmet could also be made of animal sinew. As an alternative, the poorest warriors could wear a caped hood made of leather that could be surmounted by a toothed crest or comb. The cap helmet was made of bronze for noble warriors and could sometimes be covered with scales. A bronze plate could be applied on the back of it for protection of the neck. Long-haired warriors – including the Balearic slingers – often did not use helmets, probably to show their valour; before battle they tied their hair behind the neck or gathered it in a net. The Celtiberian warriors employed the various kinds of helmet described above, but in most cases – especially those living in north-western Spain – they preferred wearing Celtic helmets of the Montefortino type (see Chapter 7 on the Celts for more details).

As mentioned above, the Iberian and Celtiberian foot soldiers belonged to two main categories: the *scutati* (heavy infantrymen) and *caetrati* (light infantrymen). Both types derived their name from the kind of shield that they employed, the oval *scutum* or the round *caetra*. The oval shield was introduced into Hispania by the Celts and thus was more common to find among the Celtiberians, having all the characteristics of the Celtic *scutum* (see Chapter 7). The *caetra* was a small round shield or buckler, made of wood and measuring anything from 30–60cm in diameter. It had metal fittings and ornaments on the external face and a large metal boss that covered a stout iron handgrip on the inside. Usually, the *caetra* was slung on a long carrying strap that was attached firmly to the forearm in combat. This kind of shield was extremely light and could also be used as a secondary weapon to punch the face of an enemy during hand-to-hand fighting. Larger round shields, always with an iron boss covering the handgrip, were also in use. Body armour in most cases consisted of round breastplates made of bronze that were strapped over fabric or leather cuirasses. The metal plates could be decorated in relief with zoomorphic or geometric designs. This kind of armour could also be worn by the lightly equipped *caetrati*. Alternatively, the poorest warriors could wear cuirasses made of hardened leather or natural materials such as padded linen or thickly woven panels of esparto grass. Corselets of chainmail or scale armour were widely used by the richest warriors, whether fighting mounted or on foot. These were short-sleeved and reached the knees. Sometimes corselets of mixed scale and mail construction were produced, with scales on the upper torso and the more flexible chainmail on the abdomen. The horses of the heavy cavalry could wear armour made of chainmail. Metal greaves, in most cases made of bronze, were often used by the heavy infantry.

Celtiberian swordsman. (*Photo and copyright by Terra Carpetana*)

Iberian warrior armed with thrusting and throwing spears. (*Photo and copyright by Terra Carpetana*)

Iberian warrior with round
shield. (*Photo and copyright by
Terra Carpetana*)

The Iberian and Celtiberian warriors used a huge variety of offensive weapons. The *scutati* and heavy cavalrymen were usually armed with conventional spears, which had wooden shafts and iron heads as well as pointed ferrules that could be fixed into the ground. As an alternative to the spear, all the Iberian and Celtiberian warriors could employ a peculiar throwing weapon that was used only in Iberia: the *soliferrum*. Designed by the excellent Celtiberian craftsmen, this was entirely made of iron (hence its Latin name of *soliferrum*). It varied in length – up to a maximum of 2m – and had a small, barbed head. When used at short range, the *soliferrum* was a very effective weapon thanks to the concentration of its great weight in the small head, meaning it could punch through shields and cuirasses quite easily. Apparently the *soliferrum*, like the Roman *pilum*, which it resembled, was mostly employed by the *scutati* together with a conventional spear. The light infantry and light cavalry preferred using simpler throwing javelins with wooden shafts and triangular iron heads. The employment of javelin thongs, wound round the shaft to impart a stabilizing spin and some additional thrust, was quite common. The main offensive weapon of the Celtiberian warriors was the *gladius hispaniensis* short sword with a straight blade, while that of the Iberian warriors was the deadly *falcata* short sword, which also had a straight blade. The *gladius hispaniensis* could be produced in two different models, the first of which is known as the 'atrophied antennae' *gladius*. This had an iron hilt drawn up into two short 'horns' ending in ball-shaped ornaments. It was an evolution of the Celtic antennae swords, which were brought to the Iberian peninsula during the sixth century BC by the migrating Celts. The second model of *gladius hispaniensis* had the same basic characteristics as the other, but it lacked the iron hilt with decorative antennae. According to the latest metallurgical studies conducted on surviving Celtiberian short swords, the *gladius* could be forged through two different manufacturing processes – either from a single piece of steel or as a composite blade. Swords produced through the first process were created from a single bloom by forging from a temperature of 1,237°C. The carbon content increased from 0.05–0.08 per cent on the handle of the sword to 0.35–0.40 per cent on the blade, from which we can deduce that some form of carburization may have been used. Swords produced with the second process were crafted by the pattern welding process from five blooms at a temperature of 1,163°C. Five strips of varying carbon content were created. The central core of the sword contained the highest concentration of carbon (0.15–0.25 per cent), while on its edges were placed four strips of low-carbon steel (with concentration of 0.05–0.07 per cent), and the whole thing was welded together by forging on the pattern of hammer blows. Each blow increased the temperature enough to create a friction weld at that spot. The forging operation, the most important part of the whole process, continued until the steel

Iberian warrior bearing a sun hat made of wicker. (*Photo and copyright by Terra Carpetana*)

Celtiberian spearman. (*Photo and copyright by Terra Carpetana*)

Celtiberian warrior armed with dagger. (*Photo and copyright by Terra Carpetana*)

was cold, producing some central annealing. When produced by welding different strips together, the *gladius* had a channel down the centre of the blade, but when made from a single piece of steel, the blade had a rhomboidal cross-section. The blade of the *gladius* was two-edged for cutting and had a tapered point for stabbing during thrusting. A solid grip on the weapon was provided by a knobbed wooden hilt added to the blade, usually with ridges for the fingers. The blade length was 60–68cm, while and overall sword length was 75–85cm. The blade was 5cm wide, and the overall weight of the weapon was about 900g.

The *falcata* was probably designed by the Iberians as a local copy of the Greek *kopis* short sword, which was brought to Iberia by the Greek colonists. It had a peculiar curved shape, widening towards the point, which was designed to move the centre of gravity further forward than in a sword with a straight blade like the *gladius*. The characteristic shape of the *falcata* increased the kinetic efficiency of its blows, this being confirmed by Diodorus Siculus, who reported that these short swords were so effective that no kind of helmet or armour could resist their strokes. Only the inside edge of the *falcata* was sharpened, so it was employed as a slashing weapon; both edges of the *gladius* were sharpened. The *gladius hispaniensis*, however, was lethal because of its point and thus was employed as a thrusting weapon. The *falcata* was produced with a process very similar to the one described above for the *gladius*, but from just three strips of varying carbon content (two hard strips, with one soft strip in the middle). The *falcata* could be manufactured with two different types of hilt with distinctive shapes: bird's head and horse's head. The hilt for both types was fitted with protection for the fingers in the form of small chains or prismatic bars. The size of the *falcata* varied around an average of about 60cm. The most common way of carrying it, like for the *gladius*, was in a scabbard made of leather or wood, which had iron reinforcements at the edges, throat and point. Metal rings attached to the edges of the scabbard allowed the warrior to sling it on a long baldric passing from the right shoulder to the left hip. In addition to their short sword, most of the Iberian and Celtiberian warriors carried short knives that could have triangular or curved blades. These were transported in a very peculiar way, since they were thrust under the framing of the sword's scabbard. Sometimes one or two 'reserve' spearheads could also be carried in this way by each heavy infantryman. The Iberian daggers with antennae hilt and triangular blade were copied by the Romans, who developed their own *pugio* from them.

The inhabitants of the Balearic Islands fought in a very distinctive way compared with the other Iberian warriors. They were all armed as slingers and were known throughout the Mediterranean world for their excellent abilities as light infantry skirmishers. The Balearic warriors' skill with the sling was developed from their early childhood, when they began intensive training at the hands of their fathers. The first toy that they were given was a sling, and according to ancient sources, as soon as a Balearic boy started to have some familiarity with his sling, a piece of bread was placed on a stake and the young trainee was not allowed to eat it until he had

Celtiberian swords and round shield. (*Photo and copyright by Terra Carpetana*)

Iberian round shields. (*Photo and copyright by Terra Carpetana*)

knocked it to the ground. The rigorous training of a Balearic slinger lasted for his entire life, as a result of which the skills of these light skirmishers were so impressive that they were more famous than any other Iberian fighters. The Balearic sling was a simple weapon in the eyes of foreigners such as the Romans, but it was capable of great accuracy. Indeed, a Balearic slinger could kill an enemy wearing metal helmet and armour from a great distance. The Balearic warriors were the first fighters from Iberia to be employed in large numbers as mercenaries by the Carthaginians, being recruited during the Sicilian Wars that were fought between Carthage and Syracuse. The sling was used as a weapon of the poor in various areas of the Mediterranean, but no slingers of Antiquity had a level of military professionalism comparable to those from the Balearics. Living on rocky islands located in the middle of the western Mediterranean, they could earn a living and improve their economic condition only by serving abroad as mercenaries. Their deadly weapon was also fundamental for their daily life, being largely employed for hunting.

A Balearic slinger used three different slings of different length and size, which were employed to throw missiles over short, medium and long distances. According

Balearic slinger.
(*Photo and copyright by Terra Carpetana*)

Balearic slinger preparing his weapon for a shot. (*Photo and copyright by Terra Carpetana*)

Balearic slinger. Note the practice of having the longest sling wrapped around the head. (*Photo and copyright by Denis Taverne of Make Carthage Great Again*)

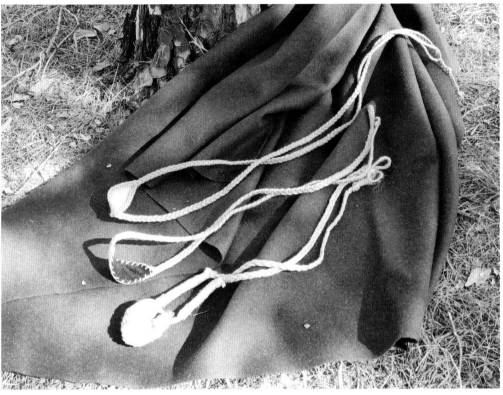

Display of Balearic slings. (*Photo and copyright by Terra Carpetana*)

to Diodorus Siculus, one sling was worn looped around the head and another around the flanks while the third one was being used. According to the first-century BC Greek historian Strabo, all three were fastened around the brow as a sort of hair-band. The Balearic slings could be made of vegetable fibres, interlaced animal tendons or animal sinew. The missiles of small and medium size were made of lead or ceramic material, while the heavier ones for longer ranges were formed from stones. Whatever their size, all were transported in leather bags. The lead missiles had an ellipsoidal shape and were poured into moulds, six or eight at a time. Most of the slingers also carried a sword and a *caetra* shield in addition to their main weapon, to be used for personal protection in hand-to-hand combat. The sling was used by the Balearic warriors while standing erect, whirling the light thong three times around their heads before launching the bullet. According to contemporary sources, the Balearic slings were capable of throwing their projectiles with such force that they seemed to have been shot from a catapult and not by a man. As a result, the Balearic slingers could be employed to perform a variety of tactical duties. They could form a screen of missile troops in front of their army's main columns, conduct reconnaissance missions, launch raids against enemy encampments, skirmish with other light troops, attack from distance heavily equipped formations, counter cavalry incursions, participate in siege operations and even cover retreats. On most occasions, including during the bloodiest of battles, the slingers from the Balearic Islands suffered very light casualties since they rarely if ever fought hand-to-hand with their enemies. Initially, the Romans hated them for this reason, considering fighting from a distance a sign of cowardice. Very soon, however, Hannibal's favoured light infantrymen also started to be admired by their enemies. Like the Cretan archers who were also employed as mercenaries by Carthage, the Balearic slingers were a unique formation in the military forces of Antiquity, being an elite unit strongly linked to their home territory and having combat capabilities that could not be copied by any other contingent. According to ancient sources, Hannibal loved practicing with the sling and had a very high opinion of the weapon. After the end of the Punic Wars, the Balearic slingers became an important component of the Roman Army, which had always suffered from a chronic lack of well-trained light troops. In dominating the Mediterranean and going on to create the Empire, Rome recruited large numbers of mercenaries from the Balearic Islands and employed them with success during campaigns conducted against various enemies.

Chapter 7

The Celts

History and organization

To understand why the warriors from Cisalpine Gaul were so effective in battle and became an important component of Hannibal's army, it is necessary to describe how the Celtic communities of the La Tène period lived and how they were organized from a social point of view. Basically, each free Celtic man was a farmer, in line with the social model of all the Indo-European peoples. Farmers made up the largest of the four categories that comprised Celtic society, the other three being the aristocracy of the rich warriors, the religious caste of the priests (the druids) and the slaves. The various farms of a settlement and the communities living in them were all grouped around a hill fort owned by a warlord, the Celtic hill forts being not only fortified places, but also the centres from which the various political leaders controlled the life of the farmers living under their control and protection. The size and extent of the fortifications were determined by the power of the aristocrats who owned them: some covered just a few acres and protected several hundred huts, while others could extend for hundreds of acres and protect thousands of huts. Defences could range from a simple rampart-and-ditch structure to much more complex defensive systems made of stone. Hill forts could be used on a permanent basis or be employed only in times of war when the population needed defence, and were generally built to protect not only the farmers but also their precious animals. The fact that the Celts were great warriors and raiders should not overshadow that they were also very capable peasants: agriculture and breeding were their main activities in peacetime, being mostly based on the production of cereals and the breeding of animals such as horses, cows, poultry and sheep. Not all Celtic free men, however, were farmers/peasants: a minority of them were artisans practicing productive activities that were fundamental for their society. The most important of these were weaving, potting, charcoal-burning and metal-smelting. Slaves could be owned by each free man, but obviously the noble warlords had larger numbers of them. Slaves were usually captured enemies and were particularly precious, because they could be employed intensively to perform every kind of labour on the farms or to help the artisans in their work. The druids were separate from the rest of the population and were probably the most important group of Celtic society. The religion of the Celts was based on their belief that the objects and natural environment surrounding them were all pervaded by magical entities, influencing the daily life of men and determining the destiny of each individual. Rituals and sacrifices were the most common practices of Celtic religion, their purpose being to placate the various magical entities in order to receive better treatment in daily life. Sacred myths and tales were extremely common and popular, being used as a tool by the druids, who took advantage of popular superstition to increase their power and influence the political life of their communities. Many of these myths and tales, based on the figures of heroic warriors and magical or natural elements, survived the collapse of the Celtic world and influenced European culture and imagery for several centuries. Religion was practiced by all members of Celtic society and was strongly linked to the daily life of farmers and warriors, with many collective rituals related to the natural agricultural seasons or to war. Deities were an important component of Celtic religion, but they were not organized according to a precise structure as for the Greeks or the Romans. As with all the Indo-European peoples, the Celts had some major gods who were respected across the whole Celtic world but also some minor deities who were strongly linked to local communities, for example being related to a river or a mountain. Most of them were usually represented as animals, which played an important part in Celtic religion, being sacred and respected. The druids were in charge of conducting all rituals and sacrifices, but also had other important functions. They were not only magicians responsible for the religious life of their community, but also judges who were called to act as arbitrators in disputes.

Blood-feuds, frequently related to the ancestry of families, were extremely common and could cause major bloodshed without the direct intervention of a priest. Apparently, thanks to their special skills and great knowledge, the druids could perform both these functions in an effective manner. They were the guardians of Celtic culture and religion, which were mostly oral and thus had to be transmitted to the younger generations in order to be preserved. The druids were thus the real rulers of the Celtic world, much more so than the rich warlords. Celtic religion included some practices that looked particularly barbarian to the Greeks and Romans, such as human sacrifice or head-hunting. Human sacrifices were common practices among various Indo-European peoples, having also been carried out by the Greeks and Romans during the early phases of their history. However, head-hunting was peculiar to the Celtic vision of the world, the Celts being convinced that the head of a man – usually a warrior – contained his personal life force, a mixture of his mind, spirit, will and strength. As a result, collecting heads of dead enemies was a way for Celtic warriors to increase their abilities, each head passing its vital energy to its new owner.

Gaul chieftain with
chainmail. (*Photo and
copyright by Historia Viva/
Confraternita del Leone*)

Gaul warrior with chainmail. (*Photo and copyright by Historia Viva/Confraternita del Leone*)

In addition to human and animal sacrifices, the Celts also practiced weapon sacrifices, consisting of votive deposits of arms and armour, especially if these were captured from a defeated enemy. Thanks to this peculiar religious practice, archaeologists have been able to find hundreds of Celtic swords in a very good state of conservation. The 'sacrificed' spoils could also include other metal tools, but weapons (together with war chariots) had a very important symbolic value. These votive deposits have been found on specifically consecrated ground as well as in lakes or marshes.

Celtic military organization changed very little during the La Tène period – which started around 450 BC – compared with that of the previous Hallstatt period. Celtic armies were never structured on regular military units like the Greek phalanxes or Roman legions. Military contingents continued to be raised according to their tribal or family origins, being strongly linked to the clan to which they belonged. When the leader of a Celtic tribe decided to go to war, all the free men living under his protection had to serve, meaning that farmers and warriors alike left their homes and assembled at the hill fort of their warlord. Some military leaders were powerful and rich enough to be named kings and thus controlled very large territories. In the event of war mobilization, all minor aristocrats living on these lands had to assemble their tribal contingents and join their overlord to form a 'royal' army. Celtic military organization was highly influenced by social structures, being based on the strong relationship existing between the upper class of the nobles and the large community of peasants and farmers. For raids or incursions against bordering tribes, free men could decide to join their warlord with the hope of looting enemy resources, but were not obliged to abandon their farms. However, in the event of full-scale foreign invasions or major expeditions of conquest, all able-bodied free individuals were required to fight. Celtic military organization was not much different from that of Feudal Europe: an army was formed of several different contingents, each led by a noble warlord who commanded his own personal retainers. A number of these could be professional fighters who earned a living as soldiers, but the majority were part-time warriors who served in exchange for protection and benefits. Each warlord commanded a different number of warriors and there were no standard tactical units: a great noble could assemble thousands of men, while a minor one could lead into battle just a few hundred followers. The overall commander of a Celtic army, which could be a king or simply the most prominent warlord, usually experienced great problems in keeping together so many ambitious military leaders and their warriors. Each tribal contingent was distinguished by its own insignia, which probably had a more symbolic function than a tactical one. This general organization became even more complex when a military expedition was organized to conquer and settle new territories, in which case the warriors would also take with them their families and

Gaul heavy infantryman.
(*Photo and copyright by Historia Viva/Confraternita del Leone*)

Gaul warrior armed with axe. (*Photo and copyright by Insubria Gaesata*)

all their goods, including animals. A Celtic campaign of conquest was effectively a mass migration that involved many thousands of individuals, the tribes being peoples on the move, with the marching warriors followed by huge numbers of wagons with their families. Keeping order and some form of organization among this mass of people was extremely difficult, which only some great military leaders were able to do.

Differently from what happened during the previous Hallstatt period, in the La Tène era Celtic armies started to include a larger variety of troop types. Although the infantry remained the most important component numerically, cavalry – including both chariots and horsemen – became increasingly decisive in the outcome of battles. The cavalry were entirely provided by the aristocracy, with warlords of superior rank mounted on chariots while minor nobles fought as simple horsemen. Chariots could be used as mobile platforms during battles, but on numerous occasions they were simply employed on the battlefield to transport nobles, who preferred to fight on foot when the enemy was deployed in close order. Chariots were effective as mobile platforms only when a battle was in its early stages (during the preliminary skirmishes carried out from a distance) or when it was over (when the defeated enemy could be attacked from the rear, transform a retreat into a rout). All nobles, either fighting on chariots or astride horses, had heavy personal equipment and wore full armour.

Gaul chieftain with leather cuirass. (*Photo and copyright by Insubria Gaesata*)

Gaul chieftain armed with throwing javelin. (*Photo and copyright by Insubria Gaesata*)

Each of them was accompanied by one or more servants, driving the war chariot or taking care of the horse. Peasants/farmers formed the infantry, the richest among them being in the first lines with their better-quality personal equipment, while the poorer ones fought as missile troops with light infantry equipment. The bow was never particularly popular as a light infantry weapon among the Celts, most of the skirmish troops instead comprising slingers and javelineers.

Celtic cavalry was excellent and of a superior level compared with the mounted contingents deployed by the Mediterranean armies: Celtic horses were not very tall or strong, but they were generally bigger than those ridden by the Greeks and Romans. In addition, Celtic horsemen were trained to charge enemy infantry by using their long slashing swords in deadly fashion. With the exception of the Macedonian cavalry of Alexander the Great, the Greeks – and also the Romans – rarely used their cavalry as a shock force with massed charges, their mounted troops being mostly employed for reconnaissance and auxiliary purposes. The Celts, however, gave great importance to the offensive capabilities of their cavalry and included large numbers of horsemen in their armies (comprising up to one-third of their strength). The cavalry numbers were so high because the nobles and professional soldiers were always mobilized in case of war, whereas the poorer individuals served as infantry only when called upon to do so for larger campaigns. Mediterranean armies were shocked by their first encounters with Celtic cavalry, the Celts being far better than any other European people at fighting on horseback, with the only exception being those from the Eurasian steppes (such as the Scythians and Sarmatians). Over time, Celtic heavy cavalry became the most famous mercenaries of the Ancient World, being employed by most of the Hellenistic armies (including that of Hannibal) and later becoming the backbone of Imperial Rome's cavalry. Coordination between infantry and cavalry did not always work in perfect fashion, usually because there we no good means by which to transmit signals or orders. While each tribal unit had its own musical instruments, these were not used like those of the Roman legions, their only function being to boost the morale of the troops and intimidate the enemy.

Equipment and tactics

Head-hunting and human sacrifices were not the only elements of the Celtic world that impressed the Greeks and Romans: they were also in awe of the physical appearance of these northern warriors, who were much taller than the average Mediterranean man of the time and had impressive musculature. Their completely white skin, blue eyes and blonde or red hair formed a combination rarely seen in southern Europe. With the daily life of an average Celtic farmer/warrior being characterized by many activities that favoured the development of a certain athleticism, some practices – like that of styling their wavy or curly hair with lime to whiten it – increased the Mediterranean perception of the Celts as wild 'creatures' from a mostly unknown world. Knowing this to be the case, Celtic warriors left their hair uncut in order to draw it back from the forehead and create the appearance of the white mane of a horse. Long beards and drooping moustaches were also very popular, together with the wearing of brightly coloured clothing, often decorated with geometric motifs which would gradually transform into a proto-Tartan. Differently from the Greeks and Romans, all Celtic men wore trousers, a revolutionary piece of clothing for the time which gave good protection from the cold during winter (something particularly appreciated in Continental Europe) but was also very comfortable to wear when riding a horse. Indeed, the Romans gradually adopted the wearing of trousers and exported their use throughout the Empire. The Mediterranean peoples were particularly impressed by the multi-coloured fabric that the Gauls used to produce their trousers, which was decorated with chequered and striped patterns that they had never seen before. During spring and summer, most of the Celtic men wore only trousers, but in the autumn and winter these were supplemented by tunics and cloaks. Tunics could have long or short sleeves, while cloaks were often partly made of fur in order to offer better protection from cold temperatures. Both the tunics and cloaks were usually ornamented with braiding and fringes in contrasting colours, which were produced separately and attached later. As was the case for arms and armours, the social status and wealth of each individual was reflected in the quality of the clothing they wore, with noble and rich warriors having tunics and cloaks with heavy decoration, while poorer peasants and farmers could afford only simple clothes in single colours and no ornamentation.

Footwear consisted of simple leather shoes, differently from the Mediterranean peoples who preferred wearing sandals. Jewels were extremely popular with the Celts and had a highly symbolic value: wearing a torque around the neck meant being a Celtic man, such a jewel being a mark of distinction in the Ancient World. These neck rings could be made of gold, silver or bronze according to the wealth of their owners, most of the golden and silver ones being decorated with highly detailed incisions. Brooches, used to fix the long cloaks around the shoulders, were another extremely common component of Celtic outfit. The practice of painting and tattooing bodies was also extremely popular. The Celts used woad (a plant) to produce a deep blue dye that was used for tattooing. Body painting on the face, arms and torso had a ritual significance and showed an individual's trust in the gods.

As mentioned above, Celtic clothing was extremely colourful and embroidered in a very peculiar way, vertical and horizontal lines forming a distinctive decorative pattern

Gaul warrior wearing leather cuirass. (*Photo and copyright by Insubria Gaesata*)

Gaul leather cuirass. (*Photo and copyright by Insubria Gaesata*)

that would later evolve to become the famous tartan. Bright colours and geometrical motifs were peculiar to the Celts, which made their clothing easily recognizable all over the Ancient World. These colours were obtained from vegetables that were unknown by the Greeks and Romans, so their use in clothing was something completely new to those living around the Mediterranean. Basically, the ordinary clothing of a Celtic man or warrior included three elements: tunic, breeches and cloak (which was heavy for winter and light for summer). These were produced in brighter colours and had extensive embroidering if worn by a rich or noble individual. Ordinary men, meanwhile, had more simple clothing. Cloaks were the most precious component of a Celtic man's wardrobe, together with the brooches that were used to keep them in position. Wool was used to manufacture winter clothing, while linen was employed for summer. Silk and gold thread was used only to decorate the dress of the richest nobles. In addition to the necklaces and brooches already described, Celtic men loved to wear other jewels such as bracelets or rings.

With the development of the La Tène cultural phase and the Celtic expansion across Europe, the panoply of Celtic warriors started to be much more varied and complex. Developing much more frequent and stable contact with other peoples, the Celts began to adopt some military elements that were characteristic of other civilizations, while at the same time starting to influence the populations fighting against them. Generally speaking, Celtic arms and armour did not change dramatically during the long La Tène era. However, analysis of surviving artefacts has made it clear that there was a slow but steady evolution. Of all the components that made up the panoply of a Celtic warrior, the helmet was probably the most peculiar. Unlike other pieces of their equipment, helmets could vary greatly since several different models were in use at the same time. At the beginning of the La Tène period, Celtic helmets could be of three different kinds: hemispherical, conical or the so-called Negau type. Hemispherical helmets were extremely simple. Produced from a single piece of bronze, they were plain, having only a simple ridge around the base. Conical helmets were much taller and could frequently have an impressively tall upper section surmounted by decorative feathers of various colours. This kind of head protection was much more costly and difficult to produce than the simple hemispherical helmet, and was frequently decorated with rich incisions on the outer surface. All this suggests that conical helmets were mostly produced for noble or rich warriors while the hemispherical ones were the standard issue for common fighters. In later periods, the hemispherical helmet would develop into the Coolus model, while the conical version would be progressively abandoned. Gradually, hemispherical helmets started to have a larger protective ridge on the back, which later expanded to become a neck guard (which was the main feature of the new Coolus model). Conical helmets like those worn during the early La Tène period were used also by other peoples of the time, their shape being perfect to avoid serious injury caused by blows from above. Apparently there were also some helmets mixing hemispherical and conical features, which was the case with the famous 'Agris Helmet' found in central France and dating back to 350 BC. Obviously a ceremonial helmet, this was entirely covered by gold foil on its outer surface and decorated with a series of rich sculpted motifs connected with pieces of coral. The Agris Helmet is vaguely conical in shape, but has a small neck guard similar to the later hemispherical helmets. It is unique among known Celtic helmets for its quality, having surely belonged to an extremely rich and important warlord. Negau helmets were a direct evolution of the previous double-ridge or Buckelhelm helmet. They consisted of a pot-shaped bottom part with a wider brim around the base. The previous transversal ridges, surmounted by a large crest made of horsehair, were initially reduced in their dimensions and later completely substituted by a single ridge (this being no longer surmounted by a crest). Negau helmets generally had little decoration, so we can suppose that they were worn by common warriors and not only by nobles. This kind of head protection was extremely popular in the Balkans, but also in Italy, being used on a large scale by important populations like the Illyrians. During the mid La Tène period, these three basic models of helmet started to be supplemented by others, which are collectively known as parade helmets: these were not employed in battle and had only a ceremonial function. They had more or less the same shape as the hemispherical or conical helmets, but were characterized by rich decorative elements. These could consist of horns (in various different shapes) or could reproduce in a stylized way the general appearance of some sacred animals. These decorations were placed on the peak of the helmet and were quite impressive, especially if the general shape of the helmet was conical. A perfect example of these parade helmets is the 'Waterloo Helmet' found in the Thames, dating back to 150 BC. This has a hemispherical shape but is characterized by two conical horns with terminal knobs. Another famous Celtic helmet with decorative horns is the 'Elmo di Casaselvatica', which is of the later Montefortino model but has two massive horns riveted on its sides. This kind of horned helmet was probably worn by the Ligurians, on whose territory the Elmo di Casaselvatica was found.

Around 300 BC, Celtic helmets started to assume their definitive conformation, with the progressive abandonment of the previous models and the creation of four new ones: Montefortino, Coolus, Agen and Port helmets. The Montefortino soon became the most popular of the four types, being used on a massive scale by Celtic warriors. It was so effective and easy to produce that it was later also adopted by the Romans, who transformed it (with a few adjustments) into the standard helmet of their legions. Its name derives from the location in central Italy where a first helmet of this kind was discovered. The Montefortino has a round shape with a raised central knob and protruding neck guard. The top was usually surmounted by coloured plumes, while the neck guard was generally decorated with incisions. Differently from previous Celtic helmets, the Montefortino has a pair of cheek pieces, which can be of two main different kinds, according to their shape. One model of cheek pieces

Gaul axeman wearing padded cuirass. (*Photo and copyright by Insubria Gaesata*)

Gaul axeman wearing leather cuirass. (*Photo and copyright by Insubria Gaesata*)

reproduced the stylized shape of the cheek, while another was trilobate, consisting of three small disks in the shape of a triangle. Apparently, trilobate cheek pieces were influenced by the contemporary helmets and armour of the Italic peoples, which frequently included this peculiar combination of three disks. Over time, however, this kind of cheek pieces was abandoned and the other type became dominant, being the one adopted by the Romans. In general terms, Montefortino helmets had many positive features: they were easy to produce, gave excellent protection to the wearer's face, could be easily decorated in many different ways and were comfortable enough to be worn for a long time. All these characteristics made the Montefortino the most popular helmet of the Celtic world. Decoration could be added in many different ways in order to transform a simple helmet into a ceremonial one. As we have already seen, decorative horns could be applied on the outer surface (like on the Elmo di Casaselvatica), while the basic central knob could be substituted by a central insert with several branches and hollow finials (on which multiple feathers could be applied). Decorations could be even more complex, like in the case of the famous 'Ciumesti Helmet' found in Romania, which has a bronze spike instead of the central knob, on which there is a cylinder crowned by a massive decorative bird. It is not known whether the bird is supposed to be a raven, an eagle or a falcon, as all three of these birds were sacred in the Celtic religion. The eyes of the bird are made of yellow ivory and have a red enamel pupil, while the wings are impressively large and are applied to the body of the bird in a peculiar way, whereby when the wearer of the runs, the wings go up and down to simulate the flight of a real bird and produce a terrible metallic noise (maybe it was meant to be a psychological weapon). Other sacred animals of the Celts reproduced on parade helmets, included boars, deer, wolves, foxes, bears, horses and bulls.

The Coolus helmet co-existed with the Montefortino version for a long time, being later adopted by the Romans on a large scale. It had a simple round shape, with a ridge running around its base and being enlarged at the back to become a neck guard, similar to the one on the Montefortino. In addition, the Coolus helmet had a couple of cheek pieces that reproduced in a stylized way the human cheek. Being extremely easy and cheap to produce, the Coolus helmet became very popular, especially with the auxiliaries of the Roman Army. According to archaeological finds, cheek pieces were added to Coolus helmets only at a later date, as a result of the Montefortino's influence. As a result, at least initially, the Coolus helmet looked more or less like a simple metal cap. Crest fittings were added by the Romans only at a later time. The Agen helmet was characterized by a wide brim on the lower edge that makes it look like a bowler hat. The general shape was hemispherical, with a prominent ridge between the main body of the helmet and the brim. Initially, Agen helmets did not have cheek pieces, but later adopted the same ones attached to Coolus ones. Unlike the latter, Agen helmets had plumes on a central knob. The characteristic brim was narrow at the front of the helmet and wide at the back; in the central part of the helmet's length, the brim was reinforced by a V-shaped section, apparently derived from the peculiar brim of Boeotian helmets used in the Hellenistic world. The Port helmet was quite similar to the Montefortino. It was round in shape and had a ridge running around its base; this ridge, on the back, expanded to become a neck guard and was reinforced by two smaller ridges. On the front, the Port helmet was characterized by the presence of embossed eyebrow decorations, which had a very practical function since they helped in deflecting blows. Cheek pieces were of the same kind applied to Coolus and Agen helmets, and there was no central nob to hold a plume. During the Roman period, the Agen and Port helmets mixed some of their main characteristics and gave birth to the famous Imperial-Gallic family of helmets.

During recent years, various aspects related to Celtic armour have been widely discussed by scholars in an attempt to find answers to the many questions that still exist regarding it. For instance, did the Celts use body armour on a large scale? Did they use leather armour or only bronze cuirasses and chainmail? And was armour used only by rich/noble warriors or also by common fighters? Finding a definitive response to these three basic questions is not easy. First of all, we should describe the Celtic concept of 'heroic nudity', which was somewhat different from that of the Greeks. Many Greek and Roman authors and artists have described or reproduced Celtic warriors as naked fighters, attacking their enemies with no personal protection and being equipped only with their offensive weapons. But should this general picture be applied to all Celtic warriors or only to a specific number of them? The answer can probably be found in some peculiar aspects of Celtic religion. A true Celtic warrior, in order to show his valour, would have marched into battle without armour and armed only with his sword. This would have demonstrated his total faith in the gods and his contempt for death. Consequently, we could plausibly assume that the presence of naked warriors in Celtic armies was probably due to some specific religious practice that was used to show a fighter's courage and religious zeal. Maybe it was a sort of initiation rite for younger warriors or a religious practice performed by some brotherhoods of warriors who had dedicated their lives to the gods. From ancient sources, for example, we know that the Gaesatae Celts frequently fought naked: maybe this was linked to their peculiar condition as mercenaries who had dedicated their entire life to war? We know that Greek and Roman writers and artists often emphasized the presence of naked warriors in Celtic armies in order to present them as wild barbarians with a lower level of civilization. Such a propaganda

Gaul light infantrymen. (*Photo and copyright by Insubria Gaesata*)

operation is clearly visible in important artistic works like the famous statue the 'Dying Galatian' from Pergamon. So, the answer to our first basic question is that the Celts used armour on a large scale, like all other peoples of Antiquity, the only exception to this rule being some specific categories of warriors who fought naked for religious reasons.

The answer to the second question is probably the most difficult one to find, as organic materials such as leather do not survive for centuries and tend to vanish with the progress of time. Metals, instead, can easily survive for very long periods, which is why we have several examples of Celtic bronze cuirasses and iron chainmail and no surviving elements of leather armour. Iconography is not of great help in answering our question, since representations of Celtic warriors with armour are extremely rare. The Celts surely did wear organic armour and not only bronze cuirasses or iron

Gaul light infantryman armed with spear and throwing javelins. (*Photo and copyright by Insubria Gaesata*)

Gaul swordsman.
(*Photo and copyright by Insubria Gaesata*)

Gaul warriors conducting a reconnaissance mission. (*Photo and copyright by Insubria Gaesata*)

chainmail, but leather or linen cuirasses were definitely not as popular as those made from metal. There were two main reasons: organic armour was not part of the Celtic military tradition, and the Celts were famous for their working of metals and not for their artefacts made from other materials. A Celtic warrior would have preferred fighting naked instead of using organic armour: indeed, for the Celts, armour was a synonym of metal, whether bronze or iron. This general concept, however, does not exclude the possibility that the Celts also employed cuirasses made of leather or linen, which were probably much more common among the eastern Celts, who were influenced by the military practices of the Greek world.

Another important consideration regarding this point brings us to the third question: organic armour was a popular alternative to metal for the poorer warriors. Noble or rich warriors were generally equipped with personal protection made of bronze or iron, but this was too costly for the common peasants and farmers, who were not professional warriors. As a result, we could say that the use of these two different kinds of armour corresponded to the economic situation of the individual warriors. The poorest ones, albeit not fighting naked, probably did not have the possibility to buy even organic armour made of leather or linen. A final consideration on this matter is of a practical nature, as wearing heavy armour made of metal was much simpler for noble warriors, since they fought on war chariots or mounted on horses. The common warrior, fighting as an infantryman, would have lost most of his mobility if wearing a bronze cuirass or iron chainmail. At the beginning of the

La Tène era, Celtic armour mostly consisted of bronze discs worn over the chest to protect that vital part of the body. These were generally decorated with incisions and bosses, being quite light and easy to wear. The practice of wearing simple discs as body protection was also very popular among other contemporary peoples, such as the Italics or Iberians. In addition, noble or rich warriors could wear padded garments covered with leather and strongly reinforced by small bosses or discs made of bronze. These were sleeveless and generally reached the knee of the wearer, and the bronze bosses and discs could sometimes have a specific disposition in order to reproduce a decorative geometrical pattern. These leather garments were frequently worn in combination with the traditional Celtic waistbelt, which was quite large and made of bronze. Bronze greaves, quite simple in shape, continued to be used, albeit not on a large scale.

Around the end of the fifth century BC, there was a revolution regarding Celtic armour: it was then that the Celts invented chainmail. This kind of armour would soon become extremely popular in the Mediterranean world, being used on a massive scale until the fall of the Roman Empire and later for most of the Middle Ages. The fact that the Celts invented the most effective and widespread kind of armour in the history of the world is another important confirmation of their absolute superiority as metal-workers. Like with their helmets, the Romans soon understood the great potential of this Celtic military invention and introduced it into their own military forces. Basically, a chainmail – known as *lorica hamata* by the Romans – is made of thousands of small iron rings linked together in order to form a mesh, the rings being strongly interlocked to create something similar to a knitted sweater. Depending on its dimensions, a chainmail is made up of around 20,000 metal rings and weighs approximately 10kg. Generally, Celtic chainmail was sleeveless but had reinforcement panels for the shoulders, which were attached across the top of the back and held at the front by a bar and stud device. A double thong was stretched from the rings attached just above the inner corners of cut-outs to the outer corner of each of the reinforcement panels. The edges of the latter were bound with rawhide, in order to create a raised border. The panels could have angled or rounded-off ends on the chest. Later Celtic chainmail started to have short sleeves, but this did not change their general shape. Around the end of the fifth century BC, while chainmail became extremely popular among the western Celts, the eastern ones started to employ organic armour made of leather or linen, clearly inspired by the cuirasses worn by contemporary Greek hoplites and phalangites (such as the famous linothorax, made from linen). This organic armour was not as effective as chainmail, but was much lighter and easier to produce. It was perfect for the hot climate of the southern Balkans and cost much less than a metal corselet. The Celts

Gaul warriors preparing an ambush. (*Photo and copyright by Insubria Gaesata*)

did not change the Greek pattern and even included pteruges (strips of leather worn together with the armour to protect the upper arms and waist) in their own sets of armour. However, they usually decorated organic armour with their own peculiar patterns, by either painting linen cuirasses or making incisions on leather versions. Generally, this organic armour had reinforcement panels for the shoulders exactly like with chainmail, the panels of which could sometimes be made of leather rather than metal rings. Chainmail or organic armour was worn over the everyday dress of a Celtic man, which was quite practical and simple. However, there was often some additional padded garment under the chainmail to protect the wearer from wounds

Gaul warriors displaying different kinds of panoply. (*Photo and copyright by Insubria Gaesata*)

caused by the breaking of the metal rings, which could happen, for example, when a chainmail was pierced by an arrow.

In addition to armour, all Celtic warriors used massive shields to protect themselves. These were also carried in battle by the poorest fighters, their use was a fundamental element of Celtic tactics together with the use of long slashing swords. Celtic shields are part of that category known as body shields because they were long and large enough to protect a warrior from the shoulders to the ankles. The oblong Celtic shields could have two different shapes – hexagonal or oval – and most of them had a central spine made of wood and a boss (umbo) made of metal, which were designed to reinforce the whole structure of the shield. Bosses were oblong and could have different shapes. Celtic shields were made of oak planks, which were chamfered to a thinner section towards the rim, while the wooden spine, swelling in the middle, was shaped in order to correspond with a round or oval cut-out in the shield's centre. The strap-type metal boss crossed over the wider section of the spine and was riveted on the external surface of the shield. The surface – either on both sides or only on the front – was entirely covered with leather that could be painted in various bright colours and have decorations of several kinds (always linked to Celtic religious beliefs). Bosses corresponded to the handle of the shield on the back, and thus had an important function in protecting the user's hand. Additional metal binding was frequently attached to the external edges of the shield in order to reinforce it. Decorative metal figures were frequently applied to the external surface, in combination with the painted decorations. Like many other elements of the Celtic panoply, the oval shields were copied and adopted by the two fiercest enemies of the Celts: both the Greeks and the Romans introduced oval shields in their armies after encountering the Celts on the field of battle. Greek armies of the Hellenistic period started to include a new category of medium infantrymen, known as *thureophoroi*, who were equipped with Celtic oval shields and had no other personal protection except for a helmet. The Romans adopted oval shields after reorganizing their legions according to the new manipular structure: the *scutum* (oval shield) continued to be employed by the Roman legions until the reign of Augustus, while the *auxilia* (most of whom were of Celtic origin) continued to use it for at least another two centuries. Celtic cavalry, especially during the second half of the La Tène period, started to have smaller and round shields instead of the oval or hexagonal ones; these were constructed according to the same system described above, but were much more practical for use in the saddle. Apparently, the cavalry could also employ a smaller version of the hexagonal shield, its general shape resembling a square and which was much shorter than the hexagonal shield carried by infantrymen. In addition to normal shields, Celtic warlords also had ceremonial ones that were not carried in battle. These had more or less the same shapes as the regular shields, but were made of wood and were entirely covered by a bronze sheet. This bronze sheet was richly adorned with sculpted motifs, decorative applications and gems. Two of these parade shields have been found in Britain: one in the River Thames at Battersea and another in the Witham in Lincolnshire.

The main offensive weapon of the Celts was the long slashing sword, which would later be adopted by the Roman cavalry (with the denomination of *spatha*). This was used by all the categories of Celtic warriors and not only by heavy cavalry. Celtic mercenaries were renowned in the Ancient World as excellent swordsmen acting as shock troops on the battlefield. The blade of the La Tène-period swords had a distinct elongated leaf shape, being double-edged and having a square-kink or shallow 'V' point (its sides being drawn at an angle of 45 degrees to the axis of the blade). The tang of these swords (the internal part of the handle, made of metal but covered with organic material) swelled sharply, to a point of greatest width just below its centre. The *ricasso* (the unsharpened length of blade just above the handle of the sword) was very short and had a notch that varied greatly in depth. Sword handles were made of wood or leather and generally had the form of an 'X', thus continuing the pattern of the previous antennae swords. The handle was completed by a pommel, which was connected to the tang thanks to a rivet-hole. The blade measured between 60–90cm in length and was by now entirely made from iron or steel. At the beginning of the La Tène period, Celtic swords generally measured 60cm and thus had more or less the same dimensions of those used by the Greeks and Romans. From the third century BC, however, its length started to increase and finally reached 90cm. At the same time as blades became longer, the points started to be increasingly rounded. This shape of the point clearly demonstrates that these weapons were used for slashing and not for thrusting. Generally, blades had a broad neck, with the greatest width being usually low down towards the point. Swords were transported in iron scabbards, richly decorated with incisions and/or bosses, the scabbards reproducing the general shape of the blade and being constructed from two plates: the front one, slightly wider than the back plate, was folded over it along the sides. Each scabbard was reinforced by a decorated band around the top and a sculpted chip at the bottom. Scabbards were generally suspended on the right hip from a sword belt made of leather or from a chain of linked iron rings (a distinctive element of the Celtic panoply). The sword was suspended on the waistbelt by means of a metal loop located on the back face of the scabbard. In addition to swords, Celtic warriors also used daggers as secondary weapons. These were very short but had quite large blades, with a central ridge acting as reinforcement, and could have different types of handle. Daggers could have very broad blades with a distinct triangular

Gaul sword. (*Photo and copyright by Insubria Gaesata*)

shape, but smaller models were also very popular. All of them had a triangular point, making them deadly weapons when used in close combat.

Spears were another important component of the Celtic warriors' personal equipment, being used as thrusting weapons by both infantrymen and cavalrymen. Their points were entirely made of iron and had an elongated shape. During the early La Tène period they were much larger, becoming smaller over time. The most common shape had its edges curving inwards from the belly of the blade to its tip. Butt spikes, which could also be made of leather, had a socketed or tanged fitting, with a ring in the top part (where they were joined with the shaft) and pointed at the bottom. An average Celtic spear was roughly 2.5m long. Apparently, the Celts also used some kinds of ceremonial spears, which were used as standards on the field of battle. These were much longer and larger than the normal spears, having points with many decorative holes and/or undulating edges. Parade spears were not the only kind of insignia employed by the Celts, there also being more conventional ones made of bronze, these usually reproducing the same sacred animals that were placed on the top of ceremonial helmets (boar, deer, wolf, fox, bear, horse and bull). Each tribal clan had its own insignia, which was strongly linked to the gods protecting the family group. It is believed that the famous eagles of the Roman legions derived from these Celtic standards. Celtic warriors also used musical instruments to communicate

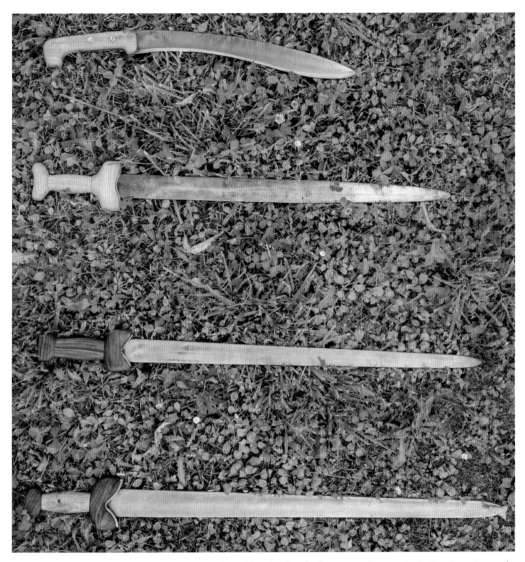

Display of different models of swords employed by the Gauls. (*Photo and copyright by Insubria Gaesata*)

tactical signals during battles: these could be traditional horns or the peculiar Celtic trumpet known as the *carnyx* (which was made of bronze, extremely long and had its mouth in the shape of a sacred animal's head). Each *carnyx* trumpet had a movable jaw and a wooden tongue, which were used to produce a raucous rattling sound. Generally speaking, Celtic warriors did not like using missile weapons. In a society that considered personal courage as the most important virtue, throwing missiles from a distance was perceived as a cowardly way of fighting. As a result of this conception, bows and slings were employed very rarely and on a small scale. Javelins were more popular and used on a larger scale, especially by the light cavalry, who rode against the enemy at the beginning of a battle and used javelins to harass their opponents. Celtic warriors preferred engaging enemies in single combat, transforming battles into a large series of duels taking place at the same time. As a result, missile weapons like bows and slings were only favoured during siege operations. Celtic light troops, both foot or mounted, were generally equipped with small round or rectangular shields with no central spine.

At the beginning of a battle, Celtic infantrymen were deployed in large masses according to their tribal/family provenance. Before charging against the enemy, they used all their psychological weapons of warfare in order to spread terror in their opponents' ranks. First of all, they slashed the air with their long swords and poured abuse on the enemy, producing a great noise with terrible war cries and by banging their weapons on their large shields. This spectacle was completed by the waving of standards and the terrific braying of horns and trumpets. During this initial phase, various champions (chosen warriors) usually came out of the ranks and engaged in duels with the best fighters of the opposing army, the outcome of these single combats often having a deep impact over the morale of the forces deployed on the field, so they cannot be seen as merely a secondary part of a battle's early phase. After these preliminary activities, the Celtic warriors charged the enemy en masse, continuing to scream and slash the air with their swords as they ran, hoping to thereby cause their opponents to panic and break up their line. Shortly before coming into contact with the first line of the enemy, Celtic warriors equipped with javelins – who were deployed in the front ranks – hurled their weapons to try to break the integrity of the enemy formation. Once in direct contact with the enemy, each Celtic warrior engaged in a duel with an opponent. These individual clashes were decided by the physique and swordsmanship of the fighters and could last anything from a few seconds to several minutes. Generally speaking, Celtic tactics were extremely simple: if the frontal assault described above was repulsed, Celtic warriors had no alternative but to launch another one. These head-on charges would continue until either the enemy army was broken or the Celtic fighters became exhausted. After a failed assault, it was common for the Celts to completely lose their morale and be crushed by an effective counter-attack mounted by their enemies. The chances of victory for a Celtic army were directly related to the success of the first charge: if this failed, Celtic warriors generally lost their impetus and were prone to abandon the battlefield in rout. The ferocious frontal assaults by the Celts caused serious problems for their enemies, including the Romans. However, Rome's armies soon learned how to stop them with javelin volleys and by alternating fresh troops in the front line.

Infantry was not the only component of Celtic armies. As we have seen, light troops – whether foot or mounted – had little tactical importance and were mostly

Gaul sword and long knife. (*Photo and copyright by Insubria Gaesata*)

Gaul knife. (*Photo and copyright by Insubria Gaesata*)

employed to harass the enemy during the early phases of a combat or during guerrilla operations conducted on broken terrain. However, heavy cavalry did play a major role in Celtic warfare, as did war chariots. The Celtic war chariot from the La Tène era was a two-wheeled vehicle with an oblong platform secured above the axle at the centre of its length. On each side of the platform were side panels formed by double semi-circular boughs of wood that were filled in with inserts of a composite material (including wood, leather and wickerwork). The trace reins were attached to the axle housing by metal lugs in order to transfer the pull directly to the wheels. The centre pole was connected both to the axle housing and to the platform. In general, due to its peculiar structure and construction, the Celtic war chariot was quite light but also stable enough to be employed on partly broken terrain. From a tactical point of view, the Celts did not use their war chariots to charge the enemy directly. Instead, these vehicles were mobile platforms from which a warlord could throw his javelins against the enemy during the early stages of combat. When the main phase of fighting began, each warlord dismounted from his chariot to fight in the front line like the other infantrymen. The servants of nobles acted as chariot drivers, transporting the weapons of their lord and taking care of the horses. Apparently, the use of war chariots was progressively abandoned in all Celtic Europe, except for the British Isles. Indeed, when Caesar's legionaries landed in southern Britain, they were greatly surprised by the presence of so many war chariots and initially had serious difficulties in combatting them. The majority of Celtic cavalrymen, being noble warriors, had heavy personal equipment including helmet and chainmail. Their offensive weapons included javelins (for use during the first phase of combat) plus spear and long slashing sword (employed during the decisive charge and in close combat). Celtic saddles were constructed with a pommel on each corner of the seat to provide a higher degree of stability. Both bar and jointed snaffled bits were used to control the horse in action.

Chapter 8

The Italic Peoples

History and organization

The Ligures were probably the first Indo-Europeans to settle in the Italian peninsula, arriving there around 2000 BC. It would be wrong to consider the Ligures only as an Italic people, because initially they lived on a vast territory that comprised most of present-day southern France as well as the entire western portion of northern Italy. During the thirteenth century BC, when new Indo-European communities arrived in Italy, the Ligures lost most of their original territories and were confined to a small strip of land located along the coastline of north-west Italy. Since those days, this region has been known as Liguria, which is mostly covered with broken and hilly terrain and is thus not well suited for agriculture. Consequently, the Ligures gradually transformed themselves into a piratical people, making a living through naval incursions. They became famous throughout the Mediterranean for their seafaring capabilities and started to be employed as mercenary warriors by several military powers of Antiquity. The Ligures fought as unarmoured light skirmishers and were very capable naval infantrymen, being used to very harsh living conditions and able to endure any kind of physical privation. With the arrival of the Celts, the Ligures lost more of their home territories and had to fight against the newcomers for their survival. Over time, however, the Gauls and the Ligures started to live together more peacefully. As a result, a new mixed culture appeared in the western part of northern Italy, which contained many Celtic as well as Ligurian elements. When Rome conquered Etruria, the Ligures acquired a border with the expanding Roman Republic. Rome fully recognized the strategic importance of Liguria, a small region with few natural resources but which connected Italy with the rest of western Europe, notably with Gaul. During the First Punic War, the Romans tried to conclude several treaties of alliance with the Ligurian tribes, but all their attempts came to nothing. The Ligures had long provided large numbers of mercenary warriors to the Carthaginians, and continued to do so also during the conflict between Carthage and Rome. In 238 BC, in response to hostile behaviour by the Ligures, the Romans launched an invasion of Liguria. On land, thanks to massive support received from the Celts, the Ligures were able to resist by using guerrilla tactics that were perfectly suited to the broken terrain on which they lived. At sea, however, the Ligurian fleet was completely destroyed by the Romans. When the Second Punic War broke out, some Ligurian tribes fought on Rome's side, but the majority of them joined Hannibal in his invasion of Italy. When the Carthaginians eventually abandoned the peninsula, the Romans occupied Liguria with strong military forces, but the Ligures were able to put up a ferocious resistance against the invaders due to the backing that they continued to receive from Carthage. During the long period from 197–155 BC, they fought the Romans using hit-and-run tactics, obtaining numerous local successes. The Ligures retreated back to the most inhospitable mountains and hills of their homeland, where it was practically impossible for the Romans to track them down without running the risk of being ambushed. More than 50,000 Ligurian prisoners were taken by the Romans and moved to other areas of Italy in an attempt to bring the guerrilla war to an end. In the long run, these harsh methods of repression worked, all the Ligurian tribes being gradually forced to surrender. By 155 BC, Liguria was under full Roman control and could be used by the expanding Republic as the main base for its operations directed against southern Gaul.

The Samnites were among the deadliest enemies of the Romans, their great military capabilities obliging Rome to reform its armies by adopting the new manipular system. The Samnites practiced transhumance, a type of semi-nomadic pastoralism that was carried out along the Appennines and which characterized the economy and society of several Italic peoples. By moving across the mountains of central and southern Italy with their livestock, they had acquired an in-depth knowledge of all the inland routes and the most important passes. Unlike the sedentary peoples living around them, the Samnites could easily move and transport most of their goods and were thus very difficult to defeat by using traditional military tactics. They were known for their love of freedom by all the other Italic peoples and were also famed for their austere way of life. A Samnite boy was taught to fight against their enemies from childhood in order to defend his sheep from raiders or wild animals. The small villages of the Samnites were usually built near major mountain passes or rivers, since control of the land routes and natural resources was fundamental for the inhabitants of Samnium. The Samnites comprised four different tribes: the Caudini, who lived in the area of present-day Benevento; the Irpini, who were settled in the area of present-day Avellino; the Pentri, who lived in the southern half of Molise; and the Carricini, who inhabited the northern half of Molise. There was also another minor tribe, the Frentani, who lived between the Marsi in the north and the Samnites in the south but had much more in common with the latter. The four main tribes made up the Samnite League, which was expanded with the inclusion of the Frentani by

Various warriors of the Carthaginian Army during the First Punic War (from left to right): Sicilian slinger, Sardinian swordsman and Carthaginian heavy infantryman. (*Colour plate by Benedetto Esposito*)

the time of the Samnite Wars. After the end of this long-running series of conflicts, despite eventually having been decisively defeated, the Samnites rebelled against the Romans on several occasions and caused serious trouble for the Republic. During the invasions of both Pyrrhus and Hannibal, the warlike Oscans from Samnium joined the foreign armies fighting against Rome, provided thousands of excellent warriors to the Epirote and Carthaginian forces. On both occasions, however, the defeat of the invaders resulted in a harsh repression of the Italic peoples who had abandoned Rome, with many Samnite villages destroyed and thousands of their civilians transferred by the Romans to other parts of Italy.

The Samnite Army was structured on *manipuli* of 200 men each, which were usually assembled in pairs so the basic Samnite unit usually comprised some 400 warriors. Each *cohors*, i.e. each couple of *manipuli*, was deployed in two lines: the first comprised of warriors equipped with javelins, while the second had men armed with a spear. It appears that there was no difference in the equipment carried by the various *manipuli*, since all Samnite fighters had several javelins and one spear as their main offensive weapons. When deployed in battle, however, the members of a *cohors*' first line were required to use their throwing weapons, while those of the second line had to adopt a more static formation by employing their spears. In practice, the second line either covered the retreat of the first line in case of defeat or advanced in close formation in case of success. If needed, a single *manipulus* could be broken into two *centuriae* of 100 men each in order to have a higher degree of mobility on broken terrain. In addition to the regular *manipuli*, the Samnite Army included a very large special corps known as the *Legio Linteata*. This chosen unit was composed of only veteran warriors who had extensive combat experience, comprising 16,000 men and thus forming an important part of the Samnite Army. The members of the *Legio Linteata* publicly devoted their lives to the main gods of Samnite religion, according to a practice known as *devotio*: a sacred oath made inside a special fence, which had a roof made of linen (hence the adjective *linteata*). Once becoming a member of this corps, a Samnite warrior served his gods and his community as a soldier for the rest of his life. Cowardice and desertion were punished with immediate death. If one of their comrades betrayed the homeland, members of the *Legio Linteata* could kill him without fear of reprisal. Executions were conducted in front of the community in order to show everyone the rigidity of Samnite military discipline. According to contemporary sources, the *Legio Linteata* was a permanent military unit and thus also served full-time in peacetime. Differently from the rest of the Samnite Army, which was mobilized only in the event of war, this chosen unit was made up of professional soldiers with superior training. The warriors of the *Legio Linteata* mostly came from the most prominent families of Samnium and had their own peculiar equipment, which comprised a silver helmet and armour. Their tunics and shields were white, with the result that the *Legio Linteata* could be easily distinguished from other Samnite units. This special corps was divided into ten sub-units of 1,600 men each, with four *cohortes* of 400 warriors in each. As a result, the *Legio Linteata* had more or less the numerical consistency of a Roman consular army of four legions. On the field of battle, it was deployed on the right wing of the Samnite Army.

Spearman of the Ligures. (*Photo and copyright by Antichi Popoli*)

As we have seen, the Greeks started to colonize the coast of southern Italy during the eighth century BC and founded several cities in the region. During the following decades, the Greek communities in the peninsula flourished and became a significant commercial power. The interior areas of southern Italy, however, were never colonized by the Greeks due to strong resistance by the local Oscan peoples, who – similarly to the Samnites in many ways – represented a strong military threat for the Greeks until Rome conquered the urban centres of *Magna Grecia*. There were three main Oscan peoples of southern Italy (in addition to the Samnites): the Campanians, Lucanians and Bruttii. In addition to these, the region was inhabited by another Indo-European population whose origins can be traced back to the southern Balkans and whose culture was similar to that of the Illyrians: the Apulians or Iapygians, who lived in present-day Puglia. The Campanians lived in one of the most fertile regions of Italy, known as *Campania Felix*, and were famous for their excellent cavalry, who were considered to be the best in the peninsula. They inhabited several smaller centres but also had a major city, Capua, which, until the Punic Wars, had roughly the same demographic and economic importance as Rome. With the arrival of the Greeks and the emergence of the Etruscans, the Campanians had to renounce most of their coastal territories, which were occupied by the newcomers. The Campanians did not have a fleet and thus could do little to repulse enemy incursions from the sea. During the fifth century BC, however, they organized a massive counter-offensive against the Greeks and Etruscans. The city of Cuma, the most important Greek centre in Campania, was occupied in 421 BC, and the Etruscan strongholds around Naples were also conquered. This Campanian renaissance, however, did not last long due to the ascendancy of the Samnites, whose main political objective was to conquer *Campania Felix*. Possession of Capua was the main cause of the outbreak of the First Samnite War, after which the Campanians and their capital city became one of Rome's most trusted allies, providing large amounts of manpower to the *alae sociorum* ('units of allies'). Nevertheless, during the Second Punic War the Campanians rebelled against Rome and joined the Carthaginians, transforming the city of Capua into Hannibal's main base in Italy. With the defeat of Hannibal, however, the Campanian territory was reconquered by the Romans and lost any kind of autonomy.

The Lucanians lived in the internal regions of southern Italy located south of Samnium. From the beginning, they tried to limit the expansionism of the Greek colonies and thus were considered as the worst enemies of the Greeks. The Lucanians obtained some notable successes against the colonists, besieging and conquering some of their most important urban centres, for example the present-day Paestum. Judging from contemporary sources, the Lucanian warriors fought exactly like their Samnite neighbours, like whom they were used to moving rapidly across the mountain terrain

Archer of the Umbrians.
(*Photo and copyright by
Antichi Popoli*)

of the Appennines. Around the beginning of the fourth century BC, the Lucanians formed a strong military alliance with the Greek city of Syracuse, the dominant power of Sicily, which sought to damage its rival Greek cities in mainland southern Italy. Having an enemy in common, the Lucanians and Syracusans collaborated on several occasions and obtained some important victories. Thanks to the help received from Syracuse, the Lucanians conquered most of present-day Calabria and thus reached the southern tip of mainland Italy. At this point the Syracusans started to change their opinion about the Lucanians, appreciating that their allies could soon become a menace to their hegemony over Sicily. Trying to limit the power of the Lucanians, the Syracusans fomented a revolt among the slaves of their former allies. The Lucanians, during their recent campaigns of conquest, had captured thousands of enemies but were too few to control them. The resulting civil war had devastating effects for the Lucanians, producing a new population: the Bruttii. These were the former slaves who had revolted against their masters and become independent from the Lucanians. The Bruttii soon occupied all the Calabrian lands that had recently been conquered by the Lucanians, greatly reducing the extent of their homeland. After the violent separation described above, the Lucanians and Bruttii endured differing destinies. The Lucanians continued their long struggle against the Greek cities of southern Italy and attacked Taras, threatening it on several occasions. To resist, the Tarantines had no choice but to ask for military assistance from their motherland: Sparta, from where the first colonists had come to found Taras, subsequently sent troops to fight against the Lucanians. Later, in 323 BC, the Tarantines had to plead for help again in order to repulse a fresh Lucanian offensive, this time receiving support from Alexander I of Epirus, uncle of Alexander the Great and predecessor of Pyrrhus. The first Epirote campaign in southern Italy, however, was a failure. Fearing that the newcomers would remain in Italy, the Lucanians and Bruttii put aside their differences and concluded a treaty of alliance, joining forces to defeat Alexander I, who died in combat during the expedition. A generation later, the Lucanians joined forces with an Epirote army and fought under the command of Pyrrhus as part of a large alliance that also comprised the Bruttii and the city of Taras. When this alliance was defeated by the Romans, the Lucanians were forced to become allies of Rome. Like the Samnites, however, they soon started preparing for a general revolt against their conquerors. Their opportunity came with the arrival of Hannibal in Italy, but when the Carthaginians were defeated the Lucanians were harshly punished by the Romans, like all the other Italic peoples who had rebelled. The Bruttii, meanwhile, after becoming an independent people, started to live as mountaineers and shepherds in the Apennines of Calabria. Here they built several small villages, which were united in a federation known as the *Confoederatio Bruttiorum*, having as its capital Consentia (the only major urban centre of the Bruttii). After joining Pyrrhus and being defeated, the Bruttii followed the same destiny as the Lucanians: they supported Hannibal during the Second Punic War, but after the victory of the Roman Republic they had no choice but to submit to the Romans.

The Apulians lived in present-day Puglia, a region of southern Italy where the territory consists almost entirely of fertile plains and where the important city of Taras is located. Thanks to their high levels of agricultural production, notably of grain, the Apulians became rich and their civilization was one of the most flourishing in Italy. As already mentioned, they were Indo-Europeans of Illyrian stock and originally came from the southern Balkans. After crossing the Adriatic, they settled in Puglia and established themselves in tribes on their new territory. The Apulians comprised three main communities: the Dauni, who settled in northern Puglia; the Peucezi, who were established in central Puglia; and the Messapi, for whom southern Puglia became their home. The Apulians built several rural settlements in their new homeland and became famous for the quality of their horses, comparable to those of the Campanians. With the ascendancy of Taras, the Apulian tribes started to experience various problems. Over time, the Dauni began to be heavily influenced by the Samnites who lived on their western borders, thereby acquiring several features that were typical of the Oscans. With the arrival of Alexander I of Epirus, however, many of their lands were conquered by Taras and they thus decided to ask for military help from Rome in order to regain their independence. In 327 BC, the Dauni concluded an alliance with the Romans and sided with them during most of the following conflicts. In the Second Punic War, however, they abandoned the Roman Republic and joined forces with Hannibal. After the Carthaginian defeat, the northern part of Puglia was permanently occupied by Rome in 194 BC. The Peucezi and the Messapi, bordering with Taras, had formed a military alliance in order to stop the expansionism of the Greek city. In 473 BC, thanks to the superiority of their cavalry, they obtained a great victory over the Tarantines. During the following decades, with substantial support from the Lucanians, they continued to attack the territory of Taras in an attempt to slow down the city's expansion. With the arrival of Alexander I of Epirus, however, the Peucezi and the Messapi were finally defeated by the Tarantines. As allies of Taras, they then took part in the campaigns of Pyrrhus, but when he was defeated by the Romans their territory was conquered by the Republic along with that of the Tarantines.

The Greeks started to colonize Italy during the eighth century BC as a result of the demographic boom in their homeland, which obliged many communities to leave mainland Greece in search of new territory where to settle. Italy, an extremely fertile land close to the west coast of Greece, soon became the most important destination

Different warriors from the peoples of central Italy (from left to right): warrior of the Picentes, warrior of the Oscans and warrior of the Umbrians. (*Colour plate by Benedetto Esposito*)

for emigrants from the various cities of Greece. Within a few decades, the Greek colonies of Italy started to flourish and became even richer than most of the cities in mainland Greece, having more natural resources at their disposal and thus being able to greatly enlarge their populations. The Greeks maintained a permanent presence in southern Italy, most notably in Sicily. Two cities – Taras and Syracuse – subsequently became dominant in Magna Grecia and later challenged Rome for possession of various strategically important territories. The Greek colonies in Sicily were even richer than those in mainland southern Italy, but had to face an enemy that was much more powerful than the Italic tribes. Since 734 BC, the Phoenicians had started to found their own colonies in the western part of the island. When these came under the political leadership of Carthage, Syracuse and the other Greek cities started to fight several wars against them in order to limit their expansionist ambitions. It soon became clear that Carthage wanted to conquer the whole of Sicily in order to control the most important commercial routes of the Mediterranean. Syracuse, being the most important and richest of all the Greek colonies on the island, was the main target of the Carthaginians. The city had been founded by the Corinthians in 733 BC, its population quickly booming. Due to the constant menace represented by foreign invaders, Syracuse was mostly ruled by tyrants, with only very short periods of democratic government. Only tyrants had the personal authority to stand up to the Carthaginians effectively. One of the most important battles fought by the Syracusans against the Carthaginians was at Himera in 480 BC, which ended in a great victory for the Sicilians. The Carthaginians, however, were not the only enemies of Syracuse: in 415 BC, during the Peloponnesian War, the Athenians organized a massive naval expedition to conquer Sicily. Against all the odds, however, the Syracusans were able to prevail in the ensuing campaign, capturing thousands of Athenian soldiers who were later employed as slaves in the city's huge mines for the rest of their lives.

The two most successful tyrants of Syracuse were Agathokles (who ruled from 317–289 BC) and Hieron (270–215 BC), both of whom tried to expand the power of their city over the other Greek colonies of Sicily and at the same time clashed with the Carthaginians. During the First Punic War, Syracuse acted as an ally of Rome, but it sided with Carthage in the Second Punic War and was finally conquered by the Romans in 212 BC after an epic siege (during which the war machines created by the Syracusan inventor Archimedes caused serious difficulties to the attackers). The Syracusan Army was mostly composed of mercenaries by the beginning of the Hellenistic period, the former citizen-soldiers who had defeated the Athenians during the Peloponnesian War becoming only a distant memory. Due to the increasing wealth derived from commerce, the tyrants of Syracuse preferred recruiting large bodies of mercenaries instead of obliging their citizens to serve (which they feared could have caused the outbreak of revolts), particularly from the reign of Dionysius I (405–367 BC). Syracuse, thanks to its strong economy, was the only Greek colony in Sicily that could maintain an entire army of mercenaries. Indeed, along with the Carthaginians, the Syracusans recruited the best mercenaries of the western Mediterranean from a variety of sources. The Syracusan mercenaries usually served in distinct units formed according to their nationality, being commanded by their own

Different kinds of Samnite warriors (from left to right): heavy cavalryman, soldier of the *Legio Linteata* and heavy infantryman. (*Colour plate by Benedetto Esposito*)

officers and equipped in their native style. At the time of Agathokles, the Syracusan army on campaign could field some 3,500 Syracusan hoplites, 2,500 allied hoplites (sent by other Greek cities of Sicily), 1,000 chosen mercenary hoplites (Greeks who formed Agathokles' personal guard), 1,000 Samnite mercenaries, 1,000 Etruscan mercenaries, 1,000 Gallic mercenaries, 500 missile troops (archers or slingers) and 800 cavalrymen. With these impressive forces, Agathokles even managed to launch a military campaign in North Africa in 310 BC with the objective of conquering Carthage, but the effort ended in failure.

In many respects, the Syracusan army was a private military force (*hetairia*) serving the tyrant who was currently in power. At its heart was the 1,000 chosen mercenaries, a permanent corps of professional soldiers who served under every tyrant. Mercenaries came from other sources in addition to those listed above, and could include the following: Cretan archers, Sicels (Italic native inhabitants of Sicily), Iberians, Ligures and other Oscans (Lucanians and Bruttii). The Oscans, in particular, were known for their incredible valour and great cruelty in battle. Many of them, at the end of their period of service, decided to remain in Sicily and form their own settlements or military colonies. Like the Tarantines, who invented a new category of light cavalry, the Syracusans also created a new troop type – the *Hamippoi*. These were introduced by Gelon of Syracuse and later exported to mainland Greece before the Peloponnesian War. The Syracusan army contained a large number of cavalry, which unlike what happened in Greece were more important than the hoplites and were an elite force. From 490–480 BC, the Greeks of Sicily fought a war against the Carthaginians, during which, in order to support his numerous horsemen against the Carthaginian heavy cavalry, Gelon created a new category of light infantrymen initially known as *Hippodromoi Psiloi*, or *Psiloi* who ran alongside the cavalry. Later simply known as *Hamippoi*, they were Psiloi light infantry who had specific equipment and training. This was derived from their peculiar tactical function: they ran into battle behind the horse of a cavalryman and held onto its tail or mane. In battle, they slipped underneath the horses of the enemy cavalry and ripped open their mounts' bellies. As a result, they were equipped with a short dagger to stab the enemy horses and were trained to run for long distances with the cavalry. Like all the *Psiloi*, they had no body armour and simply wore a felt hat. In theory, each cavalryman should have been supported by one *Hamippos*, but this only rarely happened.

Since 1600 BC, the population of Sardinia had developed an advanced culture known as the Nuragic civilization, named after the massive nuraghe towers that were built in great numbers in every corner of the island. The Sardinians lived in isolated settlements not much bigger than a village and were all shepherds, so their economy was a very simple one. However, they were experts at working metals and

Samnite warrior. (*Photo and copyright by Historia Viva/Confraternita del Leone*)

Lucanian warrior. (*Photo and copyright by Hetairoi*)

had commercial contacts with the other peoples of the Mediterranean. Around the ninth century BC, the first Phoenician colonists reached Sardinia and started to build outposts on the coast of the island. Like the Etruscans in Corsica, the Phoenicians wanted to use Sardinia as a base for their naval activities. When the various Phoenician settlements of the island came under the control of Carthage, the foreign presence in Sardinia became much more significant. The Carthaginians eventually discovered that Sardinia was full of potential mines and thus tried to penetrate the interior of the island, but met with strong resistance from local warriors who had a very warlike nature and were equipped with good quality weapons. The broken terrain of Sardinia, having no roads and being covered with hills, was perfect to organize effective resistance using guerrilla tactics. In 535 BC, the Carthaginians landed a large army on the island, but after twenty-five years of campaigning – largely involving skirmishes and ambushes – they were able to conquer only the south-western half of Sardinia. During the following decades, the Sardinians revolted on several occasions, angered by the high taxation imposed on them and the Carthaginian practice of employing them as virtual slaves to extract natural resources from the

Various warriors coming from the peoples of southern Italy (from left to right): warrior of the Lucanians, warrior of the Apulians and warrior of the Bruttians. (*Colour plate by Benedetto Esposito*)

mines. By the outbreak of the First Punic War, the portion of Sardinia that was under Carthaginian control had developed a distinctive mixed civilization, comprising both Punic and local elements. As we have seen, the Romans arrived in Sardinia after the Carthaginian garrison of mercenaries mutinied. The Sardinians resisted the Romans exactly like they had against the Carthaginians. In 215 BC, under the guidance of their great warlord Ampsicora, the whole population rebelled and attacked the Roman occupiers. Rome was at that time experiencing serious military difficulties against Hannibal in Italy, so could not send reinforcements in Sardinia. The Carthaginians, however, landed 15,000 soldiers on the island to support the rebellion. Nevertheless, Ampsicora was eventually utterly defeated by the Romans in the decisive and bloody Battle of Decimomannu, which marked the end of any Carthaginian presence in Sardinia. The local population continued for decades to wage a fierce guerrilla war against the Romans, retaining control of all the interior areas of the island, which started to be known as Barbagia ('land of the barbarians'). The Romans enslaved thousands of Sardinians and transferred them to mainland Italy in a bid to crush their resistance, but it was not until 111 BC that Sardinia was permanently pacified by the Republic.

Equipment and tactics

Ligurian warriors were all equipped as light infantrymen, with very simple arms and armour. Their panoply comprised several Celtic elements, since the Ligures came under a strong Celtic military influence well before the outbreak of the Punic Wars. Armour was not used apart from helmets, which were quite common and mostly of the Montefortino type, either with or without cheek-pieces. The main offensive weapon of the Ligurian warriors was the throwing javelin, which had a wooden shaft and triangular metal point. Each warrior of the Ligures usually carried three of these javelins. Swords, of Celtic design with antennae on the hilt, were used only by the richest warriors belonging to the aristocracy. The standard Ligurian fighter was a light skirmisher, used to moving very rapidly on the broken mountain terrain of his homeland. He was capable of walking long distances and of organizing skilful ambushes. Skirmishing from a distance and conducting rapid incursions were key elements of the Ligures' way of warfare.

The warriors of the Oscan Peoples – Samnites, Campanians, Lucanians and Bruttii – were all equipped quite similarly. Except for the fertile plains of Campania, the whole of mainland southern Italy was mostly covered with mountains, so the Oscan warriors were all equipped as medium infantry. Their panoply comprised a helmet and light armour in addition to their offensive weapons. The Oscan fighters moved

Apulian warrior (left) and Lucanian warrior (right). (*Photo and copyright by Hetairoi*)

rapidly on broken terrain in order to conduct their traditional way of mountain warfare, which consisted of guerrilla actions and hit-and-run tactics. However, they also occasionally had to confront the heavily equipped Roman legionaries, so they equipped themselves with a flexible medium panoply that could be employed to conduct raids or ambushes as well as to fight in close order against the Roman legions on open terrain. The Oscan helmets, made of bronze, could be of five different kinds: Montefortino, Chalcidian-Samnite, Italo-Corinthian, Osco-Attic and Capestrano. The Montefortino helmet was adopted following the Celts' example, while the Capestranostyle was of local design, its general shape resembling a pot with a wide brim. The Capestrano helmet – its name deriving from the place where a statue of a warrior wearing such headgear was found – was surmounted by a massive crest decorated with coloured horsehair. The Chalcidian-Samnite, Italo-Corinthian and Osco-Attic helmets were, respectively, local copies of the Chalcidian, Corinthian and Attic types produced in mainland Greece. More details on these helmets were given in the chapter covering the equipment and tactics of the Carthaginians. All the Oscan helmets were decorated with coloured crests and plumes. Oscan armour consisted of a trilobate bronze cuirass, with three disks on the front and another three on the back, each grouping having a roughly triangular shape. Four strips of bronze – two passing over the shoulders and two around the side of the torso – connected the front plate with the back plate. The Oscan trilobate cuirasses could be very simple or highly decorated, according to the economic capability of their owners. As an alternative, a simple rectangular plate of bronze could be worn on the chest, which could be very simple or reproduce the anatomy of its wearer. This kind of armour, which was worn by the poorest fighters, was held in position by four strips of leather linked on the back of the warrior. Greek-style bronze muscle cuirasses were not uncommon, but were mostly used by only the richest warriors or by a few cavalrymen. The Campanian horsemen, the only Oscan cavalry, generally had muscle cuirasses. Large waistbelts made of bronze and worn by all the Oscan warriors acted as a status symbol and were extremely precious. Bronze greaves commonly used, on most occasions worn only on the leg that was not protected by the shield. All the bronze defensive elements described above were in silver for the elite *Legio Linteata*, whose members wore white tunics. Ordinary Oscan warriors had multi-coloured tunics, decorated with geometric motifs and the outer edges in contrasting colours. Oscan shields could be of two different kinds – Argive and trapezoidal. The Argive shield was the standard round type employed by the Greek hoplites and was used by the richest Samnite warriors. The trapezoidal shield, however, was typically Oscan and was used by the great majority of the warriors, being wider in the upper part in order to protect the torso of its user and narrower at the bottom to increase the mobility of

Apulian warrior. (*Photo and copyright by Hetairoi*)

its user. In practice, the trapezoidal shield was specifically designed for mountain warfare. This kind of shield was reinforced by a central spine and sometimes could also have a classic umbo. The main offensive weapons of the Oscan warriors were the spear and the throwing javelin, which both had conventional wooden shafts and metal points. Each Oscan medium infantryman had one spear and a variable number of javelins, meaning he could fight both in close order and as a skirmisher. According to ancient sources, the Samnites were masters at striking their enemies from long distance with their missile weapons. Swords were not particularly popular, being used by only the richest warriors and the few cavalrymen; they could be Etruscan-style short swords with a straight blade or of the Greek *kopis* type with a curved blade. The Apulians, despite not being an Oscan people, were equipped with the standard Oscan panoply. Their warriors, however, made larger use of Greek defensive equipment due to their proximity to the major Greek colony of Taras. Phrygian helmets, muscle cuirasses and bronze greaves, for example, were quite common among the Apulians. Their forces, like those of the Campanians, also comprised large cavalry contingents, consisting

Lucanian warrior. (*Photo and copyright by Hetairoi*)

of heavily equipped nobles. The mounts of the Apulian and Campanian horsemen wore bronze plates for protection of the head and the chest.

Sardinian warriors used a peculiar panoply, which was quite different from that of the other Italic peoples. It should be noted, however, that over time an increasing number of noble Sardinian warriors started to equip themselves in Carthaginian fashion, with Hellenistic helmets and armour. The standard Sardinian fighter could be a swordsman or an archer; the former was armed with bronze sword and round shield, while the latter was, obviously, armed with a bow. Spears, used as a throwing weapon, were not particularly popular. All Sardinian warriors fought on foot and most of them wore the *mastruca*, a cloak made of sheepskin or goatskin, worn with the animal skin on the inside during cold months and on the outside during hot months. Almost all Sardinian warriors were shepherds, and the *mastruca* was thus the most important element of their traditional clothing. The richest Sardinian warriors protected themselves by wearing bronze disks on the chest and the back, whereas the common fighters instead wore pieces of organic armour made from the skin of the mouflon (a type of wild native sheep), which could be used to produce corselets and greaves, as well as protections for the shoulders and forearms. Collars could also be obtained from the hardened skin of the mouflon. The greaves used by the richest warriors were made of bronze. Gowns made of hardened mouflon skin were popular, especially among archers who did not have shields for personal protection. Small disks of bronze could be applied on the external surface of the usual leather armour in order to increase its resistance to blows or missiles. Most of Sardinian warriors wore helmets, which were conical in shape and could be made of bronze or hardened leather. In most cases they were decorated with two horns, which could be painted in brilliant colours or have round bronze pommels. Sardinian shields were circular and made of wood, usually having a bronze umbo in the centre, which could be used as a secondary weapon as it was pointed. Bronze plates could be applied on the external surface of shields to reinforce or decorate them. The poorest warriors had shields with just a wooden umbo. Offensive weapons included conventional spears and longbows, in addition to excellent bronze swords. The swords had straight blade and were longer than those used by the other Italic peoples. Sardinian warriors were famed for their ability to throw knives with great accuracy, each of them usually carrying three or four bronze knives attached to the back of their round shield.

Bibliography

Primary sources
Appianus, *Gallic History*
Appianus, *Hannibalic War*
Appianus, *Wars in Spain*
Cassius Dio, *Roman History*
Diodorus Siculus, *History*
Diodorus Siculus, *Library of History*
Dionysios of Halikarnassos, *Roman Antiquities*
Livy, *History of Rome from its Foundation*
Plutarch, *Lives*
Polybius, *The Histories*
Silius Italicus, *Punica*
Strabo, *Geography*

Secondary sources
Allen, S., *Celtic Warrior 300 BC–AD 100* (Osprey Publishing, 2001).
Canales, C., *El Ejército de Aníbal* (Andrea Press, 2005).
Connolly, P., *Greece and Rome at War*, (Prentice-Hall, 1981).
Connolly, P., *Hannibal and the Enemies of Rome* (Silver Burdett Press, 1979).
Fields, N., *Carthaginian Warrior 264–146 BC* (Osprey Publishing, 2010).
Hall, J.R., *Carthage at War: Punic Armies c.814–146 BC* (Pen & Sword, 2021).
Head, D., *Armies of the Macedonian and Punic Wars 359 BC to 146 BC* (Wargames Research Group, 1982).
Horsted, W., *The Numidians 300 BC–AD 300* (Osprey Publishing, 2021).
Hoyos, D., *Carthage's Other Wars: Carthaginian Warfare outside the Punic Wars against Rome* (Pen & Sword, 2019).
Newark, T., *Ancient Celts* (Concord Publications, 1997).
Newark, T., *Warlord Armies* (Concord Publications, 2004).
Quesada Sanz, F., *Armas de Grecia y Roma* (La Esfera, 2014).
Quesada Sanz, F., *Armas de la Antigua Iberia* (La Esfera, 2010).
Salimbeni, A. and D'Amato, R., *The Carthaginians 6th–2nd Century BC* (Osprey Publishing, 2014).
Salmon, E.T., *Il Sannio e i Sanniti* (Einaudi, 1995).
Sekunda, N. and Northwood, S., *Early Roman Armies* (Osprey Publishing, 1995).
Treviño, R., *Rome's Enemies (4): Spanish Armies* (Osprey Publishing, 1986).
Warry, J., *Warfare in the Classical World* (Salamander Books, 1997).
Wilcox, P., *Rome's Enemies (2): Gallic and British Celts* (Osprey Publishing, 1985).
Wise, T., *Armies of the Carthaginian Wars 265–146 BC* (Osprey Publishing, 1982).

The Re-enactors who Contributed to this Book

Make Carthage Great Again

Make Carthage Great Again is a Facebook page run by a small group of living history enthusiasts. The group began its activity in January 2022. The purpose of the page is to highlight the Punic/Carthaginian civilization through articles, photographs and information in order to underline the superior qualities of this peculiar civilization. The group is based in France and it works on the reconstruction of military life as well as of the Carthaginians' everyday life. The work of the group is based on available archaeological sources and it is aimed at highlighting Carthaginian culture through civil and military historical reconstructions. The work of photography is made as realistic as possible by working with great accuracy on the sets and landscapes and by focusing on the costumes that are reconstructed according to written primary sources.

Make Carthage Great Again est une page Facebook tenue par un petit groupe de passionnés d'histoire vivante. Le groupe commence son activité en janvier 2022. Le but de cette page est de mettre en avant la civilisation carthaginoise/punique par le biais d'articles, de photos et d'information mettant en avant la qualité de cette civilisation si particulière. Le groupe, basé en France, travaille autant sur la reconstitution de la vie de tous les jours que sur la partie militaire. Le travail est basé sur les sources archéologiques disponibles et la mise en avant de la culture carthaginoise par la reconstitution historique civile et militaire. Le travail de photographie se veut le plus réaliste possible, travaillant sur les décors et paysage pour mettre en avant le travail sur les costumes et sur les textes.

Contacts:
E-mail: denistaverne@hotmail.com
Facebook: https://www.facebook.com/profile.php?id=100077371074336&mibextid=LQQJ4d

Terra Carpetana

Terra Carpetana is a Spanish re-enactment group that was born from the interest in showing the life and culture of societies of the centre of the Iberian Peninsula; cultures that are, in some way, little known and understood. Terra Carpetana has the objective of representing these cultures, with an emphasis on accuracy, and offering to people a knowledge usually restricted to the academic field. We do this through the investigation of ancient sources and archaeological evidence that is preserved. Thanks to this, we can reconstruct aspects of these cultures such as clothing, tools, weapons and other elements that were part of their daily life. Our group is made up of people who are passionate about this era, but there are also in our ranks historians, archaeologists, teachers and re-enactors with experience in other periods of Antiquity. Some of our activities include participation in events, talks, demonstrations and collaboration with other re-enactment groups and historical, cultural or heritage institutions.

Contacts:
E-mail: contacto@terracarpetana.es
Website: www.terracarpetana.es
Facebook: https://www.facebook.com/asociacionterracarpetana

Hetairoi e.V.

Hetairoi e.V. is an association of people who have taken an interest in various aspects of ancient Greek life and culture. Our goal is to recreate as many aspects as possible of the lives of people in ancient Greece as well as in neighbouring cultures. Our chosen method is called 'living history', a concept developed out of battle re-enactments. Contrary to re-enactments, living history interpreters make use of the so-called 'third-person interpretation', where they wear recreated clothing and equipment but remain available for the audience to answer any questions and explain their activities. Sometimes, short historical scenes are re-enacted, usually narrated by a member of the group explaining to the audience what is happening. As of 2023, our members are able to show reconstructions from the early Classical era, around 500 BC, to the late Hellenistic period, around 100 BC. Because you can't fully understand a culture without studying its neighbours, we have also recreated historical impressions from the important Greek neighbours of Rome, Persia, southern Italy, Thrace and Scythia. It is very important that the reconstructed equipment and clothing are based as closely as possible on the historic originals. We strive to base our recreations on the latest scientific research and invest a lot of time in research before starting our work. If we can't craft the pieces ourselves, our reconstructed equipment is sometimes created by craftsmen who are specialized in reconstructions for museums. The Hetairoi are at your service for events in museums or educational institutions, or other events where the transfer of knowledge is the main focus. As such, we have among others already collaborated with museums like the Ephesos Museum and the Kunsthistorisches Museum in Vienna, the Reiss-Engelhorn-Museen in Mannheim, the Varusschlacht Museum und Park Kalkriese and the Historisches Museum der Pfalz in Speyer, Germany.

Contacts:
E-mail: info@hetairoi.de
Website: http://hetairoi.de
Facebook: https://www.facebook.com/Hetairoi.de

Confraternita del Leone/Historia Viva

La *Confraternita del Leone* è un'associazione culturale di ricostruzione storica, con l'obiettivo di studiare, rivivere e divulgare la storia lombarda, con particolare attenzione a quella di Brescia e delle popolazioni che l'hanno abitata nei secoli. Le ricerche dei nostri studiosi spaziano senza limiti nella ricca e complessa storia locale, concentrando l'aspetto rievocativo e didattico sui periodi dal IV al I secolo a.C. in cui furono protagonisti Reti, Celti e Romani, quindi sul secolo VIII dei Longobardi, sull'età dei Comuni e delle Signorie del XII e XIII secolo e infine sul XVII secolo e l'epoca dei Buli sotto la Repubblica di Venezia. La ricerca storica della *Confraternita del Leone* si articola su tre differenti e complementari piattaforme di studio, la cui finalità è raggiungere dei risultati di globalità analitica in grado di estrinsecare degli spaccati storici di corretta filologicità e, ove possibile, di assoluto realismo e scientificità: istituto di ricerca storica, laboratori di archeologia sperimentale e accademia di antiche arti marziali occidentali. Nel partecipare ad eventi storici la *Confraternita del Leone* allestisce un accampamento di circa 500 metri quadrati, dispone di vari antichi mestieri dimostrativi con artigiani all'opera tra cui il fabbro con la forgia, la tessitura a telaio, la macinazione di cereali, l'usbergaro, lo speziale, il cerusico, la zecca, il cambiavalute, il cacciatore, l'arcaio, lo scrivano, l'avvocato e il fabbricante di candele; in battaglia sono schierati arcieri, balestrieri, fanteria, ariete, trabucchi e mantelletti.

Contacts:
E-mail: confraternitadelleone@gmail.com
Website: http://www.confraternitaleone.com/

Antichi Popoli

L'Associazione Culturale *Antichi Popoli* nasce nel 2002 dalla passione di alcuni ragazzi per la storia e la promozione del patrimonio culturale del territorio. L'associazione attualmente cura la ricostruzione storica di tre periodi: medievale (1289–1325), etrusco (VI–IV sec. a.C.) e celtico (III–I sec. a.C.). Assieme ai suoi anni di esperienza e ricerca, può vantare anche l'iscrizione ad alcuni enti quali l'elenco regionale delle associazioni di rievocazione storica della Regione Toscana e il C.E.R.S. Il periodo etrusco prende in considerazione anni decisivi per i Tirreni, in cui ebbero luogo grandi cambiamenti nella storia di questo popolo sia per avvenimenti importanti che per nuovi assetti politici e sociali. Il periodo celtico segue la storia della Gallia Cisalpina dalla sua nascita fino all'inesorabile occupazione romana.

Contacts:
E-mail: antichipopoli@gmail.com
Website: http://www.antichipopoli.it/

Insubria Gaesata

Insubria Gaesata is a cultural association based in Milan, Italy, which focuses on the historical re-enactment of the Celtic people that lived in the northern part of Lombardy between the third and first century BC. Through constant and meticulous study and collaboration with other experts and scholars, we aim to reconstruct the history, customs, religion, warfare and every aspect related to the Cisalpine and Alpine Celts such as the Insubri and Leponzi, but also the Transalpine mercenaries known as the Gaesati. Our main objective is to spread the interest in ancient history by taking part in historical re-enactment, where we both expose the results of our studies with the aid of faithful reproductions of artefacts from the Iron Age, made by skilled artisans or by ourselves, and pique the interest of the audience with the representation of battles and duels, always striving to recreate something as close as possible to the reality of the time. Our studies so far have been focused around the topics of warfare in the Celtic world, religion and rituality, medicine – enhanced by the use of natural remedies and plants – alimentation, writing and the material culture. We do this while always making an effort to use a scientific and rigorous method, without ever falling into the suggestions offered by a certain revisionist *milieu* of the history of the Celtic period, influenced more by imaginative perceptions than by historical facts.

Contacts:
Facebook: https://www.facebook.com/InsubriaGaesata/

Index